THE
MIND
OF THE
CAT

THE
MIND
OF THE
CAT

GARY BRODSKY

Longmeadow Press

This edition is published by
Longmeadow Press
201 High Ridge Road
Stamford, CT 06904
ISBN 0-681-41018-3

Printed in the United States of America
0 9 8 7 6 5 4 3 2 1

To my four friends.

Contents

Introduction

Do you love cats? Do you share a special bond with one in particular? Imagine how special it would be if you could truly understand the mind of the cat.

Read this book and you will understand it. You will comprehend the surprising facts behind the human-like emotions a cat feels. Learn about the unique type of love that a cat can only get from a person—and the invaluable kind of rapport that one can only experience with a cat. Discover the many messages that purring can convey. Read the touching reason why cats "cruelly" play with their prey. Your cat has a complex personality—it is both aloof and dependent, domesticated and "wild," self-sufficient and yet eternally juvenile. Enter and enjoy the exciting, no-longer-secret world of your cat.

Dictionaries define "cat" as: A domesticated carnivore, widely distributed through a number of breeds. Any digitate carnivore of the family *Filidae*, as the lion, tiger, leopard, jaguar, etc., of the genus *Felis*, and the short tailed species that constitute the genus *Lynx*, and especially any of the smaller species of either genus.

Accurate as the above might be in a cold, scientific sense, it says little of the true sense and nature of the cat, the wonderful animal that now lives in more homes than any other "domesticated carnivore (or herbivores, for that matter)" in the entire world. It does not address their love or kindness, or the special wonder one finds himself living with whenever a cat enters his life.

Over the centuries, millions of people from every country in the world have praised and loved cats. People have honored them, worshipped them, treated them as members of their own family, even as their children. The cat, of course, being the noble creature it is, has taken all of this in stride.

A number of these masters have been the major poets, playwrights and authors of our time. Hundreds of them have references to cats in their major works. Many of them have also set aside special works just about their cat, or about cats in general, in an attempt to convey the special essence of what makes cats the wonderfully different animals they are. I have gathered a few of their works here in order to explore the nature of cats in brief before we get down to the heart of things later on.

"When I play with my cat, who knows but that she regards me more as a plaything than I do her?"

Montaigne

"A kitten is so flexible that she is almost double; the hind parts are equivalent to another kitten with which the forepart plays. She does not discover that her tail belongs to her until you tread upon it."

Henry David Thoreau

"Cruel, but composed and bland,
Dumb, inscrutable and grand,
So Tiberius might have sat,
Had Tiberius been a cat."

Matthew Arnold

"Lat take a cat, and forstre hym wel with milk,
And tendre flessh, and make his couche of silk,
And lay hym seen a lous go by the wal,
Anon he weyveth milk and flessh and al,
And every deyntee that is in that hous,
Swich appetit hath he to ete a mous."

Chaucer

"Self-reliant like the cat—
that takes its prey to privacy,
the mouse's limp tail hanging like a shoelace from its
    mouth."

Marianne Moore

"When I observed he was a fine cat, saying, 'why yes, Sir,
but I have had cats whom I liked better than this'; and
then as if perceiving Hodge to be out of countenance,
adding, 'but he is a very fine cat, a very fine cat indeed."

Samuel Johnson

"I'm not one o' those as can see the cat i' the dairy, an'
wonder what she's come after."

George Eliot

"The Naming of Cats is a difficult matter,
    It isn't just one of your holiday games.
At first you may think I'm as mad as a hatter,
When I tell you a cat must have THREE DIFFERENT
    NAMES.

When you notice a cat in profound meditation,

11

The reason I tell you, is always the same:
His mind is engaged in a rapt contemplation
    Of the thought, of the thought, of the thought of his
        name:
    His ineffable effable
    Effanineffable
Deep and inscrutaaable singular Name."

Of course, not every writer who ever walked the face of the earth felt the same about the noble cat. Many have had plenty to say, some of them far too much. I would like to quote here from one non-cat fancier.

The writer was Robert E. Howard. He lived from 1906 through 1936. During his relatively short life (he committed suicide at the age of 30), he created a large heap of mostly masculine stories. He brought to life an entire battalion of large-muscled characters, the most famous of these being Conan the Barbarian.

Howard was a dog lover, pure and simple. When his beloved childhood hound was sick unto death, he had to leave home and stay elsewhere until the dog finally died. So affected was he that he simply could not be present at the end.

Over the years, Howard, who lived on a farm, had quite a large number of cats due to the problems of mice, rats and larger rodents. In a letter to a friend, Howard described most of these felines by name, relating each one's individual history. He also wrote the following in a letter in my possession, which I would like to take a look at for a number of reasons.

"In his anger cries and his love cries, his gliding course through the grass, the hunger that burns shamelessly from his slitted eyes, in all his movements and actions is advertised his kinship with the wild, his tamelessness and his contempt for man.

"Inferior to the dog the cat is, nevertheless, more like human beings than is the former. For he is vain yet servile, greedy yet fastidious, lazy, lustful and selfish.

"He is monumentally selfish. In his self love he is brazen, candid and unashamed. Giving nothing in return, he demands everything—and demands it in a rasping, hungry, whining squall that seems to tremble with self-pity, and accuse the world at large of perfidy and a broken contract.

"His eyes are suspicious and avaricious, the eyes of a miser. His manner is at once arrogant and debased. He arches his back and rubs himself against humanity's leg, dirging a doleful plea, while his eyes glare threats and his claws slide convulsively in and out of their padded sheaths.

"He is inordinate in his demands, and he gives no thanks for bounty. His only religion is an unfaltering belief in the divine right of cats.

"The dog exists only for man, man exists only for cats.

"The introverted feline conceives himself to be ever the center of the universe. In his narrow skull there is no room for the finer feelings.

"Pull a drowning kitten out of the gutter and provide him with a soft cushion to sleep upon, and cream as often as he desires. Shelter, pamper and coddle him all his useless and self-centered life. What will he give you in return? He will allow you to stroke his fur; he will bestow upon you a condescending purr, after the matter of one conferring a great favor. There the evidence of his gratitude ends.

"Your house may burn over your head, thugs may break in, rape your wife, knock Uncle Theobald in the head and string you up by your thumbs to make you reveal the whereabouts of your hoarded wealth. The average dog would die in defense even of Uncle Theobald.

"But your fat and pampered feline will look on without interest; he will make no excertions in your behalf, and after the fray, will, likely as not, make a hearty meal off your unprotected corpse."

One may wonder why a book dedicated to cats would feature such a lengthy and contrary quote. I hope my answer will make sense to all of you.

The main reason for quoting the above is to try and bring as many of the non-cat lover's complaints about cats as possible out into the open. As wrong as we might feel (Okay, okay, as wrong as we know, as wrong as we know... sheesh, cat lovers can be such grouches) that Howard was in his attack, it must be admitted that he did a masterful job of attacking. I mean, let's face it—all of us—we have heard it all before.

There was a need to list all of the common diatribes most of us have suffered through so that I could then come back to them later on throughout the book. I needed all the usual nonsense nicely boxed up in one

place so that I could then dispel each of them in turn.

And, as everyone reading must know, Mr. Howard's anger, as nicely worded as it might be, is sadly misguided. There is really no more wonderful animal on the face of the earth than the cat.

I won't launch into an equally long or vicious attack on dogs just for the sake of short-sighted balance. Dogs are wonderful animals, too, and this book is not a contest. It simply comes down to the fact that the love canines are capable of giving is just not the same as that which comes from a cat. They may defend homes and children and wallets and even (oh, swoon) virginity, but they are, essentially, just loyal pack animals obeying a herd instinct as old as time.

It is surprising how many dog owners snort in derision and say that the only reason a cat stays with his owner is because he feeds it, not out of love. Dog owners do not understand that the truth is almost a complete reverse of what they believe. Oh well, enough is enough.

For now, put aside the war and all the sorry comments of the unknowing. Sit back, relax and enjoy every cat fact, secret, joke and loving story I have to share. I've been a writer for almost 20 years and yet, despite how much I love cats, it has never been dawned on me to write about them until now. Hopefully I'm not too late.

The Cat Experts

A lot of people write books without any first-hand knowledge of their subject. Childless authors write about raising children. Unmarried authors write about marriage. The list goes on and on.

This book is different. It was practically dictated to me by four true experts on feline behavior—my cats, Edward, Miranda, Clovis and Genevieve.

Edward is the oldest. The first time I saw him he was 10 weeks old and living in a pet shop cage. I was 11 and I had always wanted a cat, so I told my parents all about him. The next time we met, he was my birthday present.

He grew to be a large tabby who's an out-and-out grouch! Hint: The way to tell how big a kitten will get is to look at his paws. If he has big paws, he'll become a big cat. He tries to boss the other cats around, but they never let him. (That's probably why he's so grouchy.) He was neutered soon after his arrival, but he often reminds me of "the old man who still chases girls, but can't remember what for."

Two years after Edward's debut, I received another feline birthday present—Miranda. Miranda has a sweet, maternal personality. She mothered the two younger cats, when they were little, as though she had given birth to them.

Her special talent is fetching objects such as aluminum foil balls on command. Note: Genevieve also learned how to fetch, but neither of the males ever did.

The probable reasons could be because female felines in the wild do most of the hunting, so they—and their domestic counterparts—are much more adept at hunting, chasing, pouncing and fetching than the males.

Clovis, also a tabby, is the third. Note: Each one of the four was acquired two years apart. Why? Because every two years someone would say, "The kitten is now a cat. Let's get another kitten."—and we would. But we gave all the cats equal attention; it was in no way an "ageist" act.

Clovis is sweet and lovable. His tail was bent slightly backwards at birth and he's fat (he was neutered, too), so he often starts to roll rather than walk. He learned to roll on cue when he hears, "Roll over!" and he often does it several times for good measure. Clovis is the only one of the four who uses his paw like a hand when he eats.

One of his most frequent habits is "kneading" cushions or pillows before he settles on them for a nap. Note: Cats make "kneading" motions on objects such as pillows or blankets to simulate the way they were nursed by their mothers. Doing it gives them the same feeling that children get when they clutch teddy bears at night—a feeling of security created by a reminder of maternal love.

Genevieve is a silver tabby who has perfect markings. She stayed so small for so long that many people remarked that she had to be some kind of a "miniature cat"—and I was often asked where to buy one!

Genevieve is my favorite. And I'm her favorite human. Whenever I'm in the house, she follows me wherever I go. If I get up in the middle of the night, she gets up too. When I take her out in the backyard, she always stays near me—without a leash—and never tries to run away.

She and Miranda sit with me when I'm sick. She greets me at the door when I come home. Many times I've awakened to find that she's dropped something into my hand while I've slept. Usually it's a piece of aluminum foil. I throw it and say, "Fetch!" and she happily brings it back. She's very intelligent. I'll tell you more about her later on.

Cats' personalities can vary tremendously. Every cat has its own individual level of affection, degree of intelligence and so on. Some cats think they're dogs, and those whose owners treat them like children come to think they're human.

Note: Cats can start to believe that they're dogs or even other animals if they're raised side-by-side with them during the earliest stages of their development. Reality dawns on them eventually. Many cats reflect their owner's personality (and, very often, their owner is totally unaware of this fact).

Although Miranda usually acts sweet and passive, she doesn't hesitate to show a male who's boss if he tries to bully her. (Genevieve never tries to bully her.) Whenever she goes into action hissing and growling softly, it's hard to believe that she spends most of her time in peaceful pursuits such as purring and washing the others.

Note: Cats have a big advantage when they groom themselves—as you can see when you look at them closely, their tongues resemble sandpaper and they work as bristle brushes. They wash themselves after every meal. When they fail to wash themselves, they're probably sick. They even wash the insides of each other's ears. If you have a child who's reluctant to wash up, try pointing out a cat to him as a good role model.

While Edward was still an "only cat" a mouse happened to pay an unexpected visit. Naturally, I figured that I had the ideal "mousetrap" handy. Some mousetrap! When I aimed Edward in the direction of the mouse, I was sure that it had only moments to live. Instead, Edward took one look at it and ran away as fast as he could go. He didn't stop until he was under the bed, after meowing something that could only mean, "What's that? Get it away!"

He had never been taught to go after mice—let alone stand up to one—so his reaction was natural. House cats live according to civilized rules, not by instinct (most of the time). As Edward would say: "Of course I'm civilized! If I weren't, I would be eating cat food that's mouse-flavored, not mackerel-flavored!"

Note: An *Encyclopedia Americana* published almost 50 years ago credits cats with helping in the colonization of America. It says, "A great deal of the advance of agriculture as well as the spreading out over the vast woodland and prairies has been made possible by the domestic cat." How did the cat do this? When the pioneers were settling in America, they had to deal with 40 major groups of rodents. If they hadn't been able to deal with them, they could never have raised enough crops to survive. That's how certain furry "mousetraps" were invented. They were highly valued, and sold for $10 or $20 each—a huge amount of money in those days. The peddlers who roamed the West carried them in their carts along with pots, pans and tools.

Almost 100 years ago there was a plague of rodents in Memphis, Tennessee. A man from Arkansas supplied Memphis with cats and the plague promptly ended. And in the Disney cartoon, *Cinderella,* the heroine makes friends with amicable mice and despises the palace cat, who's depicted as mean and nasty. She would have been much better off befriending the cat and ignoring the mice, because rodents carried diseases such as the black plague in those days!

Miranda and Clovis were once locked out of the house by mistake. Far from attempting to roam the neighborhood, they spent the night by the door, waiting patiently for it to open. Their "thoughts" were obvious: "It's cold out here, and there's no cat food around! Who wants to be outside?" Further proof that house cats can become domesticated through-and-through.

Choosing Your Cat

Life with a cat (a pair of cats, a dozen...?) is a number of things. It is a joy beyond measure. Cats are vitality itself, infusing anywhere they decide to live with their infectious style. It is a life suddenly filled with companionship and an unexpected love that is unique in its depth and warmth. But, also... it is not for everyone.

My boys and girls, Edward, Miranda, Clovis and Genevieve are such a large part of my life that I literally cannot picture myself without them. But then, I grew up with cats in the house. Not that I am complaining, but I had no choice in the matter. Cats were my companions throughout my teen years simply because they were in the house. I am grateful they were there, because they turned out to be my best friends in many situations.

Now, as I've said, having cats in the house and caring for them every day seems perfectly natural to me but, that's me. I've also seen enough problems (and even a few minor disasters) involving new cat owners over the years to realize that first cats for adults who have never had one before can be a tricky situation.

Cats, one must remember, are a lot more like people than dogs. They are curious and demanding. When you are bored or busy they aren't likely to go sit in a corner just because you want them to. They must be reasoned with, as you would reason with an adult or child. Let me start at the beginning and list all of the things that should be considered before you bring a cat into your home and your life.

The first thing you must ask yourself is why you want your cat. Will it be a friend or an ornament? Do you plan to do the cat show circuit, or do you just want someone waiting for you at home? Different cats call for different degrees of care. I wouldn't suspect that someone acquiring their first cat is going to want to invest the money to purchase one of the finer pedigrees, but some beginners have been fooled into buying more high-strung breeds.

For all of you beginners, the best rule of thumb I can give is that you should simply go to one of the animal shelters in your area (believe me, no matter where you live there is going to be at least one), and look for a cat in need of a good home. Sadly, most of our country's shelters are almost always stocked to overflowing with extra cats. There really is no need to make a major investment in a fancy show animal unless that is what you plan to do with it. All cats respond to love. Taking home a shelter stray and giving it the care it has been lacking will transform it into the love of your life, as its own individual qualities come out in response.

Most shelters ask only that new owners pay vaccination and neutering fees. Between the local animal missions, and the people in your own neighborhood who are looking to find a home for kittens, you should have no problem finding a cat at an affordable price.

Of course, like any living thing, cats do not have a one time price tag. You must consider that cats need a balanced diet. Food for your cat can run between $25 and $50 a month. Kitty litter is cheap, but it has to be changed often... it may not cost much but you will use a lot of it. On top of these expenses, even if your cat is never sick, and never rushed to the vet's office for the odd emergency (it is possible, but you couldn't prove it by my bunch), there will still be the bills for the necessary vaccinations.

If you are an apartment or condo dweller, before you even start looking at cats you had better read your lease and see if pets are allowed. Nothing could be worse than falling in love with a particular cat and then being told to either get rid of it or vacate the premises.

That means you can either move out of your building, or spend the rest of your life trying to make sure no one in any of the surrounding units ever hears your cat or sees you taking kitty litter to the trash chute. The assumption being that no one who gets themselves a cat could ever bear to part with it.

It has been my experience, having raised the mixed bunch that I have, that there are no character traits predominant in either sex (which I've been able to observe, anyway). Whether neutered or not, cats are cats. There are no valid arguments for owning a cat of one sex over that of the other.

Some people will get a cat for a small child, the thought being that they have hit upon the perfect playmate for baby. Sadly, this is not really a wise plan. Cats are not very big fans of loud noises, rough handling, jerky motions, or almost any of the natural characteristics of babies and small children.

This is not to say cats and children should be kept isolated from one another until the children are teenagers. Respect for animals is much easier to instill in a small child if a cat is kept in the house with the child at an early age. But, the parents will have to spend a good deal of time teaching their child how to respect and handle the cat (if only so their child doesn't prematurely discover why kitty has its claws).

If the cat is for an adult, one consideration should be how much time will be spent with the cat. Now it is true that cats like to spend a good deal of their day (up to two thirds) at rest. They like to sleep or lounge quietly, and really don't wish to be disturbed. The other third of their day, will be active, and they will want companionship the same as any member of any other intelligent species.

This is not to say, however, that if you are an extremely busy person you should not get a cat. On the contrary. The answer is, of course, that you should get two cats! If this is the course for you, one thing to consider is trying to get two kittens from the same litter. Two cats already used to playing with each other will be easier to adjust to.

A kitten should stay with its mother for eight weeks after birth. This is a health consideration. Kittens separated too early from their mother can easily become victims of malnutrition and chronic diarrhea. If you are taking a kitten from the litter of someone you know, try to get them to keep the kitten for at least eight weeks.

As to telling a healthy kitten from a sickly one, there is no big secret. A healthy kitten is active, running, jumping and wrestling with its brothers and sisters. It will have a good appetite, clear, bright eyes and no inclination to scratch its ears (a tell-tale sign of mites). One last caution, a healthy kitten produces solid waste; diarrhea will leave the fur on a kitten's rear streaked with dirty traces. Both clean ears and clean rears are good signs that your kitten is healthy.

And that's pretty much it. If you have the patience for living with a cat, if you aren't the type to get overly excited by animals walking on top of your refrigerator, eating your house plants, scratching this or that piece of furniture, hair on your clothes and sometimes in your food, et cetera, et cetera, then welcome aboard. There is nothing more rewarding than bringing a cat into your life. Take it from one who knows!

Getting What You Want
(The Feline Way)

When it comes to the fine art of manipulation, cats are natural-born experts. For example, when Genevieve wants me to get up in the morning (to feed her) she hops onto my bureau and starts pushing something off. Amazingly, she doesn't simply knock something off in hopes of waking me with the crash. Instead, she pushes something just a few inches—and then stops and looks at me to see if I've noticed. If I haven't reacted, she pushes it just a little more and she looks at me again. If I still haven't moved, she continues to push the object until it finally falls off. And then she moves on to "Plan B."

Plan B involves jumping onto my bed, walking up to my face and poking me in the eye! If you're not easily awakened, let me tell you—that will do it. Note: I never trained her to be a "furry alarm clock." Her ideas are all her own.

One evening when Gen's dinner was a little late in coming, she took matters into her own hands, er, paws. First, she nudged open the broom closet where the cat food is kept, and pulled out a can. Because it had a plastic cover (it was the only one that did) she was able to pick it up with her teeth, and carry it down the hall. Once outside my room, she put down the can and knocked on the door with her head (which she does all the time). When I opened it, she meowed loudly. It was obvious that her meowing meant, "Feed me!...Sheesh! If only I could run the can opener by myself, I would never need you to feed me at all!"

As you can tell from these stories, one of the "secrets" of feline success (and one of the secrets of human success) is persistence. You may have heard the classic saying, "Never try to out-stubborn a cat." Remember, cats possess such incredible patience that they can watch mouse holes for hours and stay so still that birds don't notice them—until it's too late!

When cats climb up into trees, they often stay there until they're good and ready to come down. Note: If your cat gets up in a tree, don't bother calling the fire department. They always come down by themselves eventually. When they get really hungry, they "acquire the courage" to descend.

Cynics have been known to say, "Cats don't rub humans, they rub themselves against humans." This isn't true. A cat won't rub itself against you unless it likes you to begin with. When they rub up against humans (or objects they favor) they "anoint" them with a special scent (that's undetectable to humans). The scent comes from glands behind their ears, and when they share it with a human, it's comparable to sharing perfume with someone else. The action says, "You're my kind of person. You're special to me." It also serves to mark the boundaries of a cat's territory; it forms a "signboard" to inform other cats about the marker's gender.

Very often, Gen plays a game on her own which has "rules:" start at the end of the hall, race into the living room and jump to the top of the curtain rod without touching the curtains. Once you're there, balance yourself on it and walk like an acrobat on a tightrope. When she launches herself into the game, there's no stopping her. She's accomplished this feat over and over again throughout the years, and she always ends it with a look that says, "Ta-Da!"

Note: The reason behind such feline games is that cats come from a long line of skilled hunters. When they live in an environment where there's nothing to hunt, they just "hunt" anyway, even if the object of their chase is totally imaginary! Some cats are soon bored with imaginary prey. They can go so far as to grab the ankles of unsuspecting passers-by from concealed hiding places—or even leap on them unexpectedly from above. Gen often leaps to my shoulder from the floor.

Gen's run-and-leap is very similar to the chase-and-pounce of a jungle cat leaping on a gazelle or springing to a tree branch. Sometimes Miranda or Gen perches on top of the refrigerator watching everyone intently, like a concealed tiger looking for lunch. Other times she'll chase imaginary prey—halfway up the wall!

The cartoons and comic strips that depict cats fantasizing themselves into different roles are not really off-base. Walter Mitty (James Thurber's famous fantasizing character) could have been Walter Kitty.

The best way to tame your cat's antics is to play games with it that bring out its hunting instincts. Try pulling a string or a soft, safe object, such as a scurrying mouse, across the floor, or dangling it above your cat's head. Gen likes batting a small plastic ball around, and pretending to catch catnip mice. (She also enjoys ripping them apart afterwards!)

If you're away from home all day, and your cat gets so bored without your attention that she rips furniture or otherwise destroys your home, try the following:

Hide some cat treats or toys in various places around the house so that your cat will find them unexpectedly and be distracted. Just as you become less bored when you take a little break or have a small snack at work, so does your cast. Other ways to distract your cat when you're not at home include a telephone call so he can hear your voice on the answering machine, and setting the television or radio to go on at a certain time.

Cats may "travel" to the jungle by simply imagining themselves there, but they usually get what they want by more dramatic methods. Whenever Genevieve or Miranda see me getting out some luggage, they know I'll be taking a trip, so they immediately stage a "protest rally." Gen starts sharpening her claws on the sides of my bags (before I can chase her away) and Miranda starts a "sit-down strike" inside one. She plants herself firmly inside an open suitcase and, however many times she's removed, returns at once to plunk herself down again.

At such times I'm almost positive that I can hear her muttering, "Hell, no, you won't go!" I also suspect that she can make herself heavier at will. But cats can't do that—can they?

If a cat is especially angry with its owner, it can and will express this emotion by urinating or defecating where it isn't supposed to. Not only do cats sometimes

wreak their revenge this way, they also occasionally get even by soiling something they know their owner values highly. When your cat is annoyed with you, remember to hide your shoes and slippers—and anything else you leave around on the floor. Because if you don't, you may be victimized by a cat whose thought process goes something like this: "So she thinks she can talk to me that way and get away with it, eh? Watch me turn her Guccis into garbage! Ha, ha, ha!"

Another way cats try to get even with their owners is by sulking, just as humans do. I was once foolish enough to place Genevieve in a pet boarding house for a week. After her return home, she refused to "talk" to me for days! I learned my lesson. I never did it again. But before I did... She gave me the cold shoulder and turned away from me when I spoke to her. She pulled away from me when I reached to pet her. She refused to greet me when I came home. I was very relieved when she finally forgave me, because I had already made plans to purchase an appropriate apology gift—but I had no idea where to buy a 10-foot catnip mouse!

At the boarding house she wasn't put in a cage, she wasn't mistreated and she was fed her usual food—but she sulked anyway. I'm sure she was thinking, "There was no color television in that joint, the wallpaper stank and the other guests were alley cats! What a tacky place!"

I'm sure you've seen many cartoons or comic strips in which cats are shown fighting over a female. At the conclusion of the fight, the female always walks off happily with the winner. In real life, things don't always happen that way. When two tomcats start fighting over a female, the female "prize" doesn't always stick around waiting for the winner to emerge. While the fight is progressing, she often decides to wander off on her own—or, very often, with a third male! Even if she does hang around, she doesn't necessarily accept the winner's advances.

When a third male lures a female away from two combatants distracted by their fighting, his thoughts probably go something like this: "Look at those two bozos make fools of themselves! Come with me my dear, and we will enjoy an evening of refinement and romance." (Macho men take note!)

Cats generally prefer quieter methods of communication when it comes to getting what they want. Apart from the occasions when they fight, the only times that they make loud noises is when they're mating, seeking a mate or in great distress. When Genevieve is "in heat" (when she's looking for a mate) the noises she makes convey the message, "Hey there, big boy... how would you like to come up and see me sometime?"

Everyone who has ever heard her exotic-sounding, "jungle call" mating sounds is amazed that such noises could be coming from her. For one thing, she's usually very dignified, and for another, she often makes her jungle calls without appearing to make them at all. She'll often sit sedately or walk calmly while her weird wailing emerges like a ventriloquist's voice. The contrast between her dignified strolling and her wild cries could symbolize the contrast between every cat's basic animal instincts and its veneer of tameness.

You might be familiar with the cardboard cats that are sold for Halloween. The ones that depict cats with their backs arched, their fur standing on end and their tails swollen like the quills on a porcupine. What those drawings depict is some of the most impressive body language cats ever use.

When cats put their backs up and make their fur stand out, it is immensely intimidating to their opponents because those actions make them look much bigger and more ferocious and powerful. (Many female newscasters and executives wear their hair in a leonine style for much the same reason.)

When a cat merely hisses at an enemy, the low sound translates into, "So you think you can scare me, eh? You and who else? You're in real trouble now! I mean it! Leave while you can! This is absolutely your last warning!" and the like. Actual growling and screeching, which usually emerges from a fight in progress, means, "Take that! And that! I'm going to rip you to ribbons!" The sound is so frightening that it's often included on "special effects" records to create fear—which it does very well!

Many cat owners say their cat talks to them—that is, responds with a meow when they ask it a question. This type of "verbal" interchange usually occurs because the cat is seeking attention, food or something else it wants. When I ask Genevieve, "Would you like to go out?," she usually "answers" "Owwwt!" The fact that I always ask her when I'm standing by the door—and I always ask the very same question—obviously plays a part in her "comprehension" of human language.

Someone once reported to me that Genevieve spoke a two-syllable word. Even though I wasn't present on that historic occasion, I'm sure that her "word" had much more to do with the listener than with Gen's ability to articulate. The story came from a maid who had been hired to clean the house after a party. The cats had been closed in a room so that they would be out of her way, but she inadvertently opened the door. As she told me later on, "I couldn't believe my ears! As soon as I opened the door, the smallest one ran out crying, 'Mommy! Mommy'!"

Cats *are* very good at communicating. When they purr, it can mean many different things, ranging from "I am content" to "I feel sick, leave me alone." It can also mean, "I'm harmless," "I'm nervous" or, when a cat is purring to its kittens, "Don't be afraid, I'm here."

Cats can convey a wide range of feelings merely by flicking their tails. When their tails are completely upright, they may be expressing pride or curiosity. When their tails are hanging down, they may be conveying unhappiness. Sarah Bernhardt, an actress who was world-famous at the turn of the century, once said, "I wish I could have a cat's tail grafted onto the end of my spine. It would be so satisfying to lash it when I get angry!"

"My Cat Is Practically Human!"

I've heard cat owners describe their cats as practically human on many, many occasions. Let's examine the various ways that they justify this statement.

1. "My cat will accept nothing but the best! He refuses to eat anything except a certain expensive cat food, and he likes wearing his (expensive) collar."

This type of cat owner views his cat as an accessory to his own lifestyle—and as an extension of his own ego. Ironically, many of the expensive, "exclusive" cat foods that are sold are not as healthy for cats as some of the less expensive brands. When cat owners make any statement about their cat in which the word "refuses" appears, the odds are good that it is the owner who is usually very stubborn about getting what he wants. Obviously any cat who refuses to eat something will eat it sooner of later (provided it's edible) if nothing else is offered.

Note: Cats often turn their noses up at cat food simply because it's offered to them right from the refrigerator. Before you conclude that your cat is fussy, try offering it the food at room temperature. Remember that cats never stuff themselves. They prefer to eat a little at a time, and return to their feeding dish throughout the day. Always have fresh water available next to the cat's food.

When someone says, "My cat just loves his new rhinestone collar" (or his new monogrammed bowl or whatever), don't believe it. Cats are indifferent to status symbols and pricey possessions. They're just as happy with homemade toys such as pieces of aluminum foil, crumpled-up paper or safe homemade holders for catnip as they are with overpriced toys from pet boutiques.

2. "When I play the piano or sing, my cat joins right in!" Cats often respond to music from musical instruments or humans' vocal cords with noises of their own, but they don't do it to join in. They're stimulated by certain notes that remind them of mating calls or even feline distress sounds.

Over 50 years ago two doctors, named Morin and Bachrach, discovered that a certain note—E in the fourth octave—causes young cats to defecate and older ones to become excited. However, if one's singing or playing is affecting the cat, it's important to remember that a cat's ability to hear is much more acute than a human's, so it may simply be bothered by the volume.

3. "My cat can read my mind!" Genevieve often heads for the door while I'm still a block or two away from the house. This might seem like ESP (psychic ability) to some, but actually it only demonstrates how cats can distinguish footsteps much farther away than humans can.

Cat owners who believe that their cats are psychic because, for example, they run into the kitchen right after their owner thinks about feeding them, are responding by coincidence due to a desire to be fed.

To return to the subject of projecting one's personality onto one's pet, many people take this phenomenon much further and "cast" their pet as their "child" (or, alternately, many owners regard it as a "pseudo-parent").

In the classic fairy tale *Peter Pan* the family dog, Nana, is regarded as a satisfactory substitute for a human nanny (hence its name). In many families, the pet is encouraged to assume a similar protective role and become a furry embodiment of the essence of parenting. In the most dramatic instances cats have saved whole families by alerting them to the dangers of fire or leaking gas. More often, however, they serve as pseudo-parents by treating the children in the household as their kittens.

Many families that include a mature cat and a newborn baby have found that their cat is very protective of the child. Very often cats gently snuggle up to a baby as it naps and appear to purr it to sleep!

Note: Young children who are given the responsibility of caring for a pet, and are mature enough to assume such a responsibility, can derive many benefits from doing so. They often mature more quickly and develop a greater respect for living things. Children who are cruel to animals often grow up to become bullies, sadists or criminals. If you see a child abusing an animal, the child may be in need of counseling.

Couples who jointly own a pseudo-child cat together may not be ready to have children or may have decided not to have them at all. In any case, becoming pseudo-parents can prepare them emotionally for becoming parents later on, or it can simply provide them with a special emotional bond. Both parents and pseudo-parents must make joint decisions about such matters as food-buying and discipline. I've heard about more than one marriage (or dual living arrangement) that went on the rocks because one partner wanted their pet to share the bed and the other partner didn't! In many divorce cases, the biggest battle the couple has arises from the question of who gets custody of their pet!

Many singles enjoy having a pseudo-child pet. Generally, such a relationship is reinforced when a pet owner speaks baby talk to his pet or refers to himself, or herself, as "Daddy" or "Mommy" when they're alone with their pet. One cat owner I met refers to her cat as "fur child." Singles with such pseudo-children particularly appreciate that their babies can take care of themselves and that they never have to search for a baby sitter!

Unfortunately, people with pseudo-child pets often cause them to acquire their own bad habits. Many people who tend to overeat when they feel frustrated or unhappy encourage their pet to overeat with them. Very often this encouragement takes the form of comments such as the the ones parents use when they're coaxing their children to eat. For example, "Mama wants Baby to finish everything on his plate! Good boy!"—or even, "You are sooo cute—have another cookie!" Despite the stereotype of the "fat (house) cat," cats should be sleek (not thin) and energetic. Cats take many catnaps during the day, but it doesn't mean they're lazy. The brief naps that cats (and jungle felines) take originated in the jungle, where animals have to stay on the alert. There, any animal foolish enough to sleep too soundly could "wake up" inside another animal's stomach!

Note: One of the reasons for the stereotype of the fat cat (such as Garfield in the comics) is, again, a matter of personality projection. Characters such as Garfield reflect the body images of unsuccessful dieters. Garfield also reflects cynicism and greed. As with all stereotypes, cat stereotypes are perpetuated by people who don't know all the facts about a subject. Cats who get fat usually do so because they've been neutered (which doesn't necessarily cause a cat to get fat) or, once again, because their owners encourage them to overeat or feed them fattening foods.

Traveling with and without Your Cats

Traveling with cats is not easy. In almost all cases it is easier to leave them behind at home than it is to take them along with you. Let's look at all the possibilities.

First off, as everyone knows, you can simply leave a sufficient amount of food out for your cats if you are going to be gone for just a day or two. Cats are alone for eight to 12 hours a day anyway while their owners work. Yes, cats are definitely creatures of habit and they will know if you are gone for 12, 24 or 48 hours. But, as long as they don't smell smoke, and can find plenty of food and water, they aren't going to be too traumatized.

As I've said (probably more than a few times) earlier, cats are highly intelligent animals. They may not like that you are not home, and they may get a little worried. But, they are not going to have a coronary. Cats understand that if they don't like something, they can't change it. They will just go about their business and wait for you to return.

Now, the next problem is those times when you must be away from home for more than just a day or two. Cats cannot be allowed to stay by themselves for too long. A number of factors come into play, none of which you really want to deal with. Cats left alone for more than three or four days grow lonely and depressed (two states which can often lead to destruction from boredom and curiosity or revenge).

Just having a friend come by and feed the cats, even stay for an hour or two, is not enough. After a certain amount of time cats need their regular companion, or at least someone around with whom they can build a new, daily routine.

Thus your options come down to the following: either get someone to sit with the cat, leave the cat with someone else at their home (as opposed to them staying at your home), board them or take them with you. None of these alternatives are really much fun, but you have to choose one (or leave your cats home alone, which, as I said, you certainly don't want to do).

Cat sitters are the easiest of the four to deal with, but this is almost an impossibility to arrange. Truthfully, how many of your friends are going to drop everything and come and live in your house while you are gone? They have their own homes and cats to care for. Unless you are in a very special situation, this is a hard one to plan (and you certainly don't want to turn your home and cats over to a stranger who has answered an ad!).

Leaving your cats with someone else (hopefully a fellow cat lover who understands something about cats and their natures), is at least far better than leaving them alone. As I said earlier, cats are certainly creatures of routine. Taking them out of their normal environment is sure to disrupt them, but only for a few days. After that, they will pick up the routine of the household in which they are staying. Cats will be thrown off their guard for

the first few days, but at least the situation is one in which their fears will all come at the beginning and then immediately begin to diminish.

Cats, beyond all house pets, hate the idea of boarding houses. Most of them are set up in ways particularly stressful for cats. If this is your only choice (and for many people it is) then try to remember one thing: don't pick the place you like... pick the place the cat will like.

Many boarding houses for animals resemble (at least in the front room) little hotels. Menus are shown to the pet owners filled with fancy script and witty jokes, which are meant to delight owners and encourage them to leave their money and their pets and go off without a second thought. Remember, though, clever as they are... cats can't read! They don't care how talented a place is!

Don't pay for a large, pampered room. All that is to your cat is a giant box. Most cats feel much safer and more secure in a smaller, unprotected area where they can take in everything that is happening around them.

Also, another thing to think about... when you are home, you know immediately when something is wrong with your cats. You understand their individual cries and meows. Some attendant, no matter how well-trained in the field of pet care, does not. Your cat might sit with an empty water dish, a running eye, et cetera, for hours.

With this in mind, try to find a place where the cats will not be out back, or upstairs, or anywhere out of sight (and thus out of mind). Besides wanting your cats to be where the people are for safety, cats like to be where the action is. The more activity around them, the better.

Of course, this is not to say that you want to leave your furpals where all the cats are allowed to mingle. First, with no one cat actually belonging to the territory, fights for any number of reasons become very possible. And second, it only takes one sick cat to give you an entire ward filled with sick cats a few days later.

Finally, you also want to make sure that your cats are not going to be boarded somewhere near the dogs (if the particular kennel you've picked cares for both). Listening to barking, howling mutts all day and all night is not what your cats want to hear. They are lonely enough already without having to think that there is a wild dog pack waiting for them around the next bend.

Like every other aspect of finding the right boarding house for your cats, this one also has to be seen through the cats' eyes. Your cats don't know the dogs are all securely isolated. All they know is that the barking is mighty close, which is making them very uncomfortable.

Take this into consideration. Are you going to the same place over and over? If not, then you are still better off leaving the cats at home with lots of food and water (in several places just in case the water gets spilled accidentally) and someone to look in on them.

But, if you go away every weekend headed for the same destination every time, (leaving the city for the family house at the shore), then it might not be so bad to take your cats along. After the first couple of weekends they will adjust to the routine at the new household. Indeed, after the indoctrination period, the joy of having them along may make up for the trouble you had getting them there in the first place. Which leads us to the main topic of this section, traveling with your cats. This, no matter what the means of transportation, is never easy.

Cars present big problems. Unless you are going to leave your cat in a traveling case the entire time, you could be in for rough going. Cats are intelligent and curious. Some of them want to help you drive. Some just have to know what the brake and the gas pedal are. Others just love pushing the seat controls, window openers and door locks.

Now, some cats make perfect car cats, but there is no way to know what kind your cat is without getting in the car with him. Go to a parking lot or other open area and drive around to see what your cat will do.

Even if your cat is an excellent traveler, the problem of litter is still a big one. Any trip taking over two hours almost demands that you carry both a litter-filled box and water for the cat.

Note: One excellent suggestion has been made in several good cat books. When traveling with a cat, don't try to travel with a water dish. Take a chunk of ice instead. Sure, it will melt in time, but until it does, there is no mess. And, hopefully, your cat will be drinking up the melt as it runs off.

Air travel presents its own unique problems. Some airlines will allow you to ride with a cat on your lap. Some will not. Some require a health certificate, some do not. Some require that all animals ride in a cage with the passenger luggage.

Sadly, there is no way to predict individual airline policy. The airlines share no one set of rules. Your only recourse if you have to travel somewhere by air and you really want to (or have to) take your cat along, is to call the airlines (or have your travel agent do it) and find out what their individual regulations are.

Remember the following point whether in the car, on a plane, or in a hotel at the end of the trail. If you are in a strange place, and you open the door, guess who is going to make a beeline for the outside world? Yes. I'm sure you got that one right.

Some cats won't, of course. Some cats are so domesticated they won't go out the front door of their own homes. But, that is because they are territorial. They know they own the territory inside their walls, and they know someone else owns what is outside. Other cats will want to know what is outside of every place you stop.

In the end there are no easy answers to traveling with you cats or leaving them at home. For many it is heartbreaking to leave them behind, and yet it is possibly both cruel and dangerous to take them along. I have suffered through car trips with my four (my next book will be a horror novel about that never-to-be-repeated nightmare), nursed them out of the jitters after airplane rides and ridden out severe cases of the pouts when I have been forced to leave them with friends.

No matter what you do when it comes down to travel time, think things through from the perspective of your cat. Don't be fooled by people trying to sell you things designed to sound good to human beings. Make sure they are offering you something designed for the good of your cat. For both your sakes.

How to Walk Your Cat

In the popular Broadway musical, *My Fair Lady*, the main character, Professor Henry Higgins, asks, "Why can't a woman be more like a man?" When it comes to taking a cat for a walk—or rather, trying to take a cat for a walk—many cat owners are left wondering, "Why can't a cat be more like a dog?"

In other words, why can't you get a cat to walk as smoothly on a leash as dogs do? Because cats don't usually feel like walking, that's why. Seriously, it is entirely possible to train a cat to walk on a leash, as long as you go about it the right way.

Many cat owners get a sudden notion to take their cat out to impress the neighbors (both with their cat and with their ability to walk it). What happens next, most of the time, is that the moment their cat feels the collar around its neck, it starts tugging at it or simply refuses to move. If they take their cat outside and put her down, it often panics and zooms back to the house—or up a tree.

If you are training to train a cat to go for walks, follow these instructions. First of all, use a harness, not a collar. Cats don't like having their necks pulled by a collar, as a rule. Secondly, let it get used to the harness. Put it around its neck for a few hours a day inside the house for several weeks.

Note: If your cat has been leading a sheltered life—as a house cat who has never seen many strangers, let alone other animals—*gradually* introduce it to the outdoors and to other animals and people. Once you're walking it, try to avoid loud noises and strange animals.

Never attempt to drag a cat in the direction you want to go. If you do that, it will never want to walk with you. Always pull gently on the leash, and when your cat responds, reward it with praise.

The most important tip I can offer about this topic is: it's best to work with a young cat. The saying, "You can't teach an old dog new tricks" often applies to cats, too.

Cat Tricks

All animal owners like to play with their pets. But, and maybe this is only my love for my own four favorite nut cases, it seems to me there is no denying that no animal in the world is more fun to play with than a cat.

No matter what their age, most cats never lose interest in playing. Kittens with balls of string aside, the real fun that there is to be found in playing with cats usually comes when they are full grown and intelligent. Tricking kittens can certainly be amusing, of course, but it doesn't offer much in the way of excitement, unless you're into animal cruelty. Most people will drag a string along the ground for a kitten to chase, but bore of the game after a moment or two. Older cats can offer a real challenge and are much more fun to play with, especially if you just use a little bit of imagination and stay alert. The simple truth of the matter is that all cats love games.

Now, not all cats love all games. And, obviously, any game which involves their own natural instincts will be one they are sure to be more interested in. And, just like people (a phrase you can use a lot in a book like this if you are not careful), the more interested they are, the longer they will play, and the harder they will try to win.

I'd like to tell you about all the different games that each of my four like to play. Not all of them like every one of the games played in our house, of course, just like... oops... there I go again. Oh well, you get the idea. Let me get started.

Ed Ball, as you might guess, is a game that only Edward likes. Actually, I can understand that. Ed Ball is sort of a special interest activity. Of course, most of you would probably call it ping pong.

It all got started in a somewhat shameful manner. I find I am forced to admit that after seeing clips on television of ping pong playing felines, I just had to see if anyone in my brood would show an interest.

Borrowing a poorboy set (a net which attaches to any standard table, two paddles and a ball) from a friend, I set up operations on the dining room table, moving the tables against the wall so I could volley and return against it. I started paddling away, and, as I had figured, before long the constant noise (and their curiosity) had brought all of them into the room.

I thought they would watch for a while and then, maybe, one of them might get involved somehow. Much to my surprise, Edward jumped up on the table almost immediately and swatted the ball away. The others lost interest and left (maybe because they felt Edward had claimed this game as his own, or maybe because they were just not interested—it's so hard to tell), but Edward stayed, waiting for another chance to hit the ball.

To make a long story short, however, whenever I want a game I don't have to worry about a lot of preparation time. Now I can leave the table in the center of the dining room where it belongs. All I have to do is begin to erect the net. If I make a little noise while doing it, Edward is there before I have one side clamped down. Needless to say, I had to buy my own set, but it was worth it.

The Shell Game is just what you think it is. I used three halves from some old pantyhose eggs one day, and decided to try and baffle the gang. To get them to pay attention, I started playing with food. They all played along except Clovis, who just isn't a willing participant in games. I had a great time during the first game, hiding a peanut and then mixing up all three shells over and over again, until even I didn't know where the peanut had ended up. When I finally stopped one or the other or the other would swat at an egg, looking to see if they could uncover the peanut.

Miranda did the best during that first game. Since then, even though she has been beaten, she has resigned as queen of the shell game. Since then, I've used small toys, bottle caps (plastic ones, metal ones can scratch), vegetables, Miranda's aluminum foil balls and catnip balls. Edward will sometimes sit out, but Genevieve and Miranda will always play.

Water from the Sky isn't a game I would have made up myself, but I was glad to add it to our list when it was accidentally introduced. Several years ago a friend of mine came by to visit with her 10-year-old son. Falling into one of those absorbing 'old friends' conversations, the two of us got wrapped up in our chatter and began ignoring her son. Like all small boys, he found something to do on his own. What he found were my cats.

Things had been quiet for a long time until Clovis came running into the living room at her top speed (which is unclocked but impressive nonetheless) and dove onto my chair. She was followed by Miranda and

Edward seconds later. The three of them scrambled and climbed over and around me, trying to hide behind me, and generally making a bigger nuisance of themselves than usual until I finally noticed all three of them were wet. This prompted an investigation.

My friend and I found her son in the kitchen, calmly filling his squirt gun. We reprimanded and threatened the boy, who insisted, "But, ma, he likes it."

Knowing that cats can be the most contrary animals on the face of the earth, I asked him to explain (innocent until proven guilty and all that) what he meant. He pointed out Genevieve (I can forgive a 10-year-old for not knowing that 'he' was a 'she'), and told us to watch. He pointed the gun at Genevieve—she didn't move. He aimed—she still didn't move. Then, having done everything else, he fired. And missed.

Genevieve had sidestepped his shot, but rather than running in terror, she had stayed seated, calmly waiting for his next attempt. He tried again and again, but just couldn't hit her. He asked us, "See?" And we were, of course, forced to admit that, yes, we did. I asked him not to shoot the other cats, figuring that if Genevieve was having fun, why interfere?

Things went all right for the rest of the visit. My friend and her son departed, and that, I thought was the end of things. But then, several weeks later, spotting a cheap toy water gun on sale, I decided to see if Genevieve still liked the game. She did. I don't pretend to get it (I thought cats hated water), but that's the way it is with cats.

The other three still run and hide if I get out the little

pink water gun, but Genevieve will almost always play. Of course, being a cat, she almost always never gets wet!

Fishing for Cats is a game that all my cats, and all the cats I've ever met, like, and never seem to grow tired of. It is simple to prepare, easy to learn, can be played literally hour after hour after hour, and best of all, it has no winners or losers.

Use anything that can substitute for a fishing pole. An actual piece of real fishing pole works best (because of the superior flexibility), but anything similar will do in a pinch. Next (I guess obviously), get some fishing line (once again, making substitutions if you have to), and attach it to the end of your pole. Finally, attach some small rag toy to the end of the line. A simple, lightweight bundle of fabric with some trailing strips will do nicely.

The rest is simple. Just take your new gear and go fishing for cats. Believe me, that is all there is to it... throw out your line and drag your bait across the carpet. Your cats will chase it... every time... all night long.

Well, in truth I may be giving the game a little too much of the hard sell here. As we all know, cats won't do anything every time, but this comes as close to an exception as I've ever seen. If you have one of those furbuddies that just doesn't get interested in anything you try, all I can say is try one more thing. If your cat won't respond to this game, he is never going to respond to anything you ever try.

My foremost and heartiest recommendation... do not try to teach your cat any tricks. This is not to say that your cat cannot learn tricks, or that he will not, although that is often the case. Cats everywhere learn to jump up, roll over, push little carts, meow and do 1,001 other little tricks on command, to the delight of their owners and their friends. However, there is a big difference between playing games with your cat (being it's friend and play-mate) and teaching it tricks (being it's teacher), and it's a difference your cat just may not appreciate.

Dog enthusiasts love dogs for many reasons, but one of the strongest is for their ability to perform. Dogs are pack animals. Every animal in a pack has a job that they are supposed to do. Dogs are easy to teach tricks to be-cause it is part of their genetic nature to learn tasks and perform them on command.

Cats, as we all know, are not dogs. They are solitary creatures who are rarely concerned with anyone else's business except their own. Yes, out of love, out of curios-ity, out of their natural desire to play, some cats can be taught a trick or two. But they do not receive the natural satisfaction from performing that dogs do, and it simply is not worth anyone's time to try and teach a cat a trick it doesn't want to learn.

Again, as we all know, cats are extremely intelligent. They can learn to do anything they... want... to... learn—but they are going to want to have to learn it.

Now, this is not to say that if your cats start to exhibit some tendency that looks like a trick, you can't encour-age them to keep it up. Give them as many threats and words of praise that it takes to reinforce the behavior un-til they do it whenever you ask them to, but—don't try to teach them something you want them to learn unless they give you some sign that they might be inclined to do whatever it is you have in mind.

Cat's are single minded. If they don't want to learn to sit up, they won't. They will sit there and give you a look that says, "Yeah, I get it. Sit on my hind legs with my paws hanging our, begging for food. Get real. You're going to feed me anyway. You sit on your hind legs with your paws dangling out in front of you. It looks ridiculous. You want that kind of behavior... go get a dog." Then they will walk away and go back to doing whatever it is they actually enjoy.

There is also one other factor to consider. It is an exceptional dog who will get the idea in his head, "Hey, if I get a treat every time I do this trick, then I'll do this trick 10 times and I'll get 10 more treats."

Cats do not have to be very exceptional to come up with this idea. Many cats who learn tricks through the reward system will then expect a treat every time they decide to do the trick. And if they decide that time is two hours after you went to sleep, or during the middle of your favorite television show, or during Christmas dinner, then guess what, that's when they're going to do it, and that's when they're going to expect their reward.

Don't do it, friends. Don't try and turn your cats into dogs. If you want to see tricks, then go to the circus.

Cats throughout History

When Chinese ideographs (picture-writing) originated thousands of years ago, drawings of cats' eyes were included to illustrate the passage of time. Since the pupils in cats' eyes change from slits in the daytime to circles at night, the Chinese used a thin line to indicate noon and a circle to indicate midnight. The Chinese horoscope includes a cat, and in contemporary China, cats are used to predict earthquakes.

Cats, like many animals and birds, can often sense impending earthquakes do to their heightened powers of perception. During World War II, the fact that cats heard approaching missile attacks before any humans could—and headed for air raid shelters when they did—saved many lives. During World War I, cats were brought into trenches so that their sensitivity to strong odors could alert sailors and soldiers to enemy gas attacks.

Pope Leo the XII allowed a cat named Micetto to spend much of his time reclining on a fold of his papal robe. Since Leo means lion, it only seems appropriate.

During the 18th century a star was named Felis (which means cat in Latin) by astronomer Joseph Lalande.

One of the most famous cat stories in history is the one about the Prophet Mohammed, the founder of the

Moslem religion, and his cat, Muezza. Mohammed was about to respond to a priest's call to prayer when he noticed that his cat had fallen asleep on his sleeve. Rather than wake him, he cut off the sleeve! As a result of this kind gesture, cats were held in the highest esteem by Moslems for a long time afterwards.

Many famous generals and leaders renowned for their bravery were afraid of cats! Julius Caesar was terrified whenever he saw a cat, and entrusted an aide with the responsibility of keeping them away from his tent. Napoleon Bonaparte once called frantically for help, drawing his sword, when he found a tiny kitten had invaded his quarters!

In William Shakespeare's *Romeo and Juliet*, Mercutio (Romeo's best friend) insults Tybalt (Juliet's cousin) by calling him "Prince of Cats." This insult—intended to mean "Prince of Nothing Much"—refers to a fairy-tale feline with a name similar to Tybalt, who was familiar to Shakespeare's audiences.

Another very famous cat story—this time focusing on a cat's devotion to its owner—took place in the 17th century. Henry Wriothesley (otherwise known as the third Earl of Southampton) was imprisoned in the Tower of London for suspected treason. Amazingly, his pet cat made its way to his cell by climbing around the Tower, finally getting to him through a chimney. This story includes two equally strong elements of the feline personality—affection and determination.

Fascinating Facts about Cats

Cats, horses and camels are among the very few animals in the world that move their front and hind legs together when they walk.

Cats that wander off the ship to explore strange ports often rely on their boat's whistles as the signal to return. During World War II, ship whistles were silenced in port for security reasons, so many cats were left stranded!

All kittens have blue eyes before they're 3 weeks old. Cats can see the colors blue and green, but not red. They use their whiskers (among other things) to tell if prey is dead. A cat with a mouse in its mouth touches it with its whiskers to see whether it's still moving, and if it's safe to put it down.

Rapid Eye Movement (REM) in humans is a sleep in which the mind is supposedly programmed with information about one's recent activities. Cats experience the same kind of sleep. You can tell when your cat is experiencing REM when you see its paws, tail, ears and, of course, eyes twitching.

One of the women who played the villainess Catwoman on *Batman*, a popular show in the 60s, was the actress Eartha Kitt. The catwoman character had henchmen with names such as Angora and Manz, and drove a special vehicle called the Kitty Car. Her crimes always had cat connections, and she often said, "That's purr-fect!" Despite the fact that she was a criminal, Batman was attracted to her (in both the television series and in the first Batman movie); In the Batman comic book he actually married her (after she had paid her debt to society by serving a prison term).

In Japan house cats are referred to as "the tiger that eats from your hand."

Cats have the largest eyes of any mammal in relation to their body size.

Mark Twain once said, "If a man could be crossed with a cat, it would improve the man but deteriorate the cat." He kept 19 cats at his Connecticut home.

A particularly well-quoted comment about cats was made during the 16th century by Michel de Montaigne. In his collection of essays he asked, "When I am playing with my cat, who knows whether she has more sport in dallying with me than I have in gaming with her?" That's still a good question.

In *The Cat*, a famous novel written by the French author Colette, a young bride competes with her husband's cat for his love—and loses.

Although he was left-handed, Albert Schweitzer occasionally wrote with his right hand because his cat, Sizi, liked to sleep on his left arm.

Cats are often born with extra toes.

Princess Michael of Kent is the only member of the present royal family who posed for an official photograph with her pet cat (a Siamese).

The ruins of the Coliseum in Rome is home to scores of stray cats.

In a year, the average cat eats 20 times its own weight in food.

A cat's memory can be up to 200 times more retentive than a dog's.

It has been scientifically proven that stroking cats can lower one's blood pressure.

Many insane people become calmer when they're around cats.

Cats are brought to hospitals and nursing homes by volunteers to cheer up patients, ranging from children to the elderly.

A gorilla named Koko, famed for his ability to learn sign language, was given a pet kitten, whom he adored. Koko always handled it gently, and when it was accidentally run over, he was very upset. He was given a second kitten which he cared for just as much.

For years, one Manhattan resident "walked" his pet cats in Central Park by pulling a rope attached to a mini-bicycle and a wagon, in which they rode (without being attached).

Theodore Roosevelt had many cats. When one stretched out in the hall during a White House dinner, he simply made his important guests walk around it.

Villains in two separate James Bond films are shown with white cats, whom they pet while contemplating nefarious deeds (as always).

Walt Disney's feline characters are both good and bad. His good cat characters include a kitten, Figaro, who accompanies his owner everywhere (even inside a whale's mouth!) in *Pinocchio*, and the entire cast of *The Aristocats*. The villain in that cartoon is the butler, who wants to stop the lady of the house from leaving all her money to her cats.

Disney's nasty cat characters include Si and Am, the destructive Siamese cats in *Lady and the Tramp*, and the cat in *Cinderella*, Lucifer. Lucifer's chief "crime" is a penchant for eliminating mice!

The Special Bond between You and Your Cat

Many cat experts agree that receiving affection and care from a human often causes a cat to revert to juvenile behavior. This happens because the care reminds them of their kitten days, and simply because it eliminates the need for them to become "adult." Cats, however, have too much innate dignity to ever revert completely to juvenile ways and they always act more or less mature.

Cats haven't been domesticated by humans for too many years, relatively speaking, so every house cat has genetic "memories" of its wilder ancestors. In the wild (and in many alleys) cats face tough competition for food and territory, and that's when their more primitive instincts come in handy. The rapport that you and your cat share is special indeed, because it is unlike any relationship that a cat ever has, or ever can experience with other felines.

If you ever come home from a tough day at an office full of ruthless competitors, then you know how your cat feels when it relaxes with you. Similar to the friendships that can only be enjoyed by two humans who are never in direct competition, friendships between humans and cats are completely devoid of tension—on both sides. People often use their pet cats as their confidants, telling them secrets that no one else hears. Many pet owners regularly tell their pets about the events of their work days (and all the details about their relationships)—and many cry only in the presence of their pet.

Talking to your cat actually does enhance the emotional bond between you. Cats are always receptive to more attention, for one thing, and people automatically become more attached to those who hear their most intimate secrets.

When Sigmund Freud pioneered modern psychotherapy, he instructed psychiatrists to turn the couches away from themselves because he knew if psychiatric patients looked at their doctors while they spoke, many would develop strong "crushes" on them. In all likelihood, he deduced this fact after analyzing the reasons behind the creation of confessional booths.

Note: If your cat brings you a dead rodent or bird, you should be flattered, not disgusted. Praise your cat (and throw out the body when he's not looking). If your cat brings you "food" of this nature, it means that he regards you as a member of his family and someone worthy of being cared for. It is a very high compliment indeed.

Seven Ways to Keep Your Cat Alive and Well

1. Many popular house and garden plants are poisonous to cats. Keep your cat away from the following plants and flowers (and be careful about bringing them into the house): lilies of the valley, carnations, mistletoe, narcissus flowers, hyacinths, cacti, primroses, horse chestnut leaves and flowers, yew leaves, jimson weeds, larkspur flowers, castor bean, hemlock and nightshade plants.

Don't be upset if you see your cat eating ordinary grass and vomiting it up. Cats instinctively eat grass and eliminate it to rid themselves of hairballs (balls of hair that accumulate in their stomachs when they groom themselves). Vomiting is a minor matter to cats. It bothers them about as much as yawning bothers humans.

2. Never put a flea collar that fastens with a buckle on your cat. The collar may get caught on something and cause your cat to strangle. Replace the buckle with velcro, a snap or something similar.

3. If you have a balcony on which your cat relaxes, make it accident-proof by "fencing" it with some type of mesh.

4. Have your cats neutered. Tomcats tend to roam, and when they do, they often get run over, into fights or "catnapped."

Neutered females often live longer than unspayed ones. The operation eliminates the possibility of their developing certain serious conditions, and it removes the risk of their bearing too many litters.

5. Start by picking out a healthy, active kitten. Don't get one younger than 2 months old, because that is the minimum amount of time a kitten needs to be with its mother. If you have a litter of kittens to choose from, watch them for a while and pick a playful one. Many people choose "the one in the corner who looks sad" because they sympathize with the underdog—I mean undercat—but such "sadness" is usually sickness.

6. Adult cats don't necessarily need to drink milk. Just as many adult humans develop lactose intolerance (the inability to benefit from drinking milk), so can adult cats. If milk causes your cat to develop diarrhea, give it only water.

7. Never give your cat poultry bones. They can splinter and become lodged in its mouth or throat.

The Feline Breeds

The "Adam and Eve" of the feline world were cats that protected the granaries of the ancient Egyptians from rodents. Although felines existed in the wild long before then, it was at that time that the domesticated cat—today's house cat—began to "evolve."

There are a large variety of breeds recognized by the Cat Fanciers' Association (the largest cat association in America). The natural breeds they recognize are the Abyssinian, American Shorthair, Egyptian Mau, Japanese Bobtail, Maine Coon, Manx, Persian, Russian Blue, Turkish Angora and Siamese. The established breeds are the Balinese, Birman, British Shorthair, Burmese, Havana Brown, Korat and Somali. The mutations are the American Wirehair, Rex and Scottish Fold. The hybrids are Bombay, Colorpoint Shorthair, Exotic Shorthair, Himalayan and Oriental Shorthair.

Some of the more unusual breeds are the Manx, which can have either a small stump of a tail or no tail at all, and the Balinese, which has been called "the long-haired Siamese." Tabby cats (my favorite) are divided into the following four groups: Abyssinian tabbies (without markings), mackerel, spotted and classic tabbies.

Note: If you are interested in obtaining a Persian cat, remember that blue-eyed Persians are very often deaf from birth (as a result of linked genes).

The following are assorted facts about pedigreed cats:

White Persians are descended from Angoras, many of which were kept as pets by women in Constantinople harems.

Blue Persians were first recognized as a breed at the Crystal Palace show held in London in 1888. However, the Blue Persian is one of the newest Persian varieties. It has only been recognized in America since 1962.

The Black Smoke Persian has one of the oldest pedigree backgrounds. It was first written up around 1860.

There is a legend involving the Birman cat and a Kattah (that name certainly sounds appropriate!) priest of Indochina. Supposedly, the priest was murdered by robbers in front of a statue of the goddess of reincarnation, Tsun-Kyan-Kse. This act was supposed to have changed his cat to resemble the goddess, giving it eyes as blue as hers and fur as golden as the goddess' skin.

Curly-haired Devon Rex cats originated with a curly-haired kitten born in Devonshire, England. It is one of the breeds that resulted from unexpected genetic mutations.

The name Manx comes from the Isle of Man. This is the European isle where the cats first appeared.

The Korat cat originated in Thailand (formerly Siam) where it plays a part in many cultural traditions, and is

regarded as an omen of good fortune.

The first breeding pair of Siamese cats arrived in England in 1884. Siamese cats often make sounds like a crying baby.

Sphinx cats are hairless (as is the Sphinx).

The following are assorted facts about wild felines: Snow leopards are the only big cats that cannot roar.

Lionesses always stay with the pride (group) but males become loners when they reach maturity. Prides usually include from one to six mature males. Lions can mate with other big cats, and several zoos throughout the world have "combination cats" such as "ligers" (lion/tiger mixtures).

Cheetahs can run up to 65 miles an hour. They were used by Egyptians as symbols of bravery and as "hunting cats" around 1200 B.C.

There is actually a wild cat known as "the finishing cat." Although most cats dislike water, this one actually swims frequently to catch fish. This fish-catching wonder is the Bengali mach-bagral. Nature supplied it with extra-long claws, which it uses like fish hooks! Besides fish, it also dines on birds, frogs and small mammals, and it is found in Nepal, Burma, Southern China, Taiwan, Sumatra and parts of India.

Leopards prefer solitude—unless it's mating season or they're raising cubs.

Feral Cats

Feral cats are domesticated cats that have become wild, their descendants or the descendants of stray cats. Unfortunately, heartless people abandon cats in the city and the country all the time, rather than find them new homes. Often, they're laboring under the delusion that a cat's natural instincts can instantly transform a pampered pet into a self-sufficient stray.

Abandoned cats and strays usually meet with horrible deaths. They are often run over or otherwise accidentally killed. Sometimes they die of malnutrition or exposure, or from being attacked by another cat or a dog. Those that live are often sick or injured, and, of course, there is no one around to bring them to a veterinarian.

If you can no longer care for a kitten or cat, don't abandon it! Bring it to an animal shelter. There are many shelters that find good homes for all the pets in their care. If you abandon a pet, you are condemning it to a life of hardship—not a fantasy world of "freedom" and unleashed jungle instincts.

A certain seafood restaurant by a marina was once a mecca for stray cats. Many flocked to its garbage cans to dine on fish heads and leftovers from the restaurant's dinners. Many people abandoned their cats near the restaurant because they believed that the cats there led pleasurable lives.

Honestly—how would you like to eat from a garbage can at every meal? How would you like to have to fight over each scrap of food you got? How thrilled would you be to have to live in the open air, with no shelter but a few pieces of cardboard—if you're lucky?

Some people think that if they abandon a cat in a "good spot" the odds are that some kind person will eventually adopt it. The truth behind this myth is that the longer cats have to fend for themselves (and deal with a merciless environment) the less they trust humans. If someone tries to approach an abandoned cat with the idea of adopting it, the cat usually objects violently. Kindness is seldom a match for no-holds-barred hissing, spitting and scratching. (Most often, the cat simply hides whenever humans approach it.)

My parents knew all of the above when they spotted some young kittens among the "seafood cats." They were positive, however, that they could tame one of the (apparently) cute and cuddly little bundles of fur and turn it into a house cat. But this was not to be.

They managed to corner a kitten (which was hissing, spitting and scratching) and get it into their car. As soon as they put it down on the seat, it vanished into the car's interior but they decided to let it "relax" while they drove home. After they drove the car into the garage, they sat quietly in it and listened for sounds that would help them locate the little cat.

There wasn't a sound. Not a meow, not a peep, nothing. After quietly sitting in the car for a long time, they put some cat food in a dish on the back seat and left the car "empty." When they checked the back seat again, the cat food was gone, but there was no sign of the cat. They took turns sitting in the car straining their ears for the slightest rustle but they heard nothing.

They put more food on the back seat, and a litter box there, too. The cat food disappeared, the litter box was used, but there was no sign of the kitten. This went on for several days. Incredibly, the kitten was already so feral (and so frightened) at its young age, that it was able to stay absolutely silent "indefinitely."

Finally, a humane animal trap was placed on the back seat, baited with food. The next time they looked in the car, they found the kitten in the cage. They brought it into the house, but it hissed, spat and growled, not acting "kittenish" in the least.

At last they put the cage in the car, and drove back to the marina. They opened the car doors, opened the cage and got out of the car. The kitten jumped out and ran back to the group. A few months later, the restaurant closed and the cats were never seen again.

More Fascinating Facts about Cats

No, you haven't been imagining it—some cats can indeed smile. They can't grin as the Cheshire cat in *Alice in Wonderland* does, but they can manage small smiles. If you think your cat sometimes greets you with a smile, you're probably right.

When cats drink, their tongues scoop the liquid up backwards.

When cats spot potential prey that is out of their reach, they often express frustration by chattering their teeth at it. Very often, when Genevieve watches birds from a window, she moves her mouth as though she's crunching something. At such times, she seems to be thinking, "The first robin of spring! I can almost taste it!" Cat experts disagree about the reason behind such a response. Perhaps cats do it to enhance a prey-catching fantasy that prepares them for their next opportunity.

Note: Contrary to what many people believe, cats are seldom able to catch wild birds (unless they're weak). A healthy bird's ability to fly is such an advantage that it's very difficult for a cat to catch it off-guard. The fact that cats occasionally do manage to catch birds is a tribute to their truly special hunting skills.

In the year 1347, the infamous black plague struck the

Italian city of Messina. It is ironic that the second city hit by the horrific disease was called catania. Soon afterwards it spread to Florence, Venice and many other cities. By the time it had passed through Italy, one-third of the population had died from it. By the year 1351, one-third of Europe's population had succumbed to it.

The plague was conveyed by rats that carried infected fleas. Cats could easily have eliminated the rats and changed the course of history—but there were few of them in Europe at that time. The reason for their scarcity was superstition.

In those days, there were many superstitions that linked cats with evil. Scores of cats had been killed because of these beliefs—with, and without, men and women also accused of being involved with witchcraft. It is one of history's greatest ironies that the plague disaster was indirectly caused by people who believed they were avoiding misfortune. Cats are now the most popular pet in the United States. Fifty four million cats live in 26 million American homes.

Despite the evidence of all those Tarzan movies we watched, not all tigers live in the tropics. The Siberian tiger actually treads the cold and snowy forests of northern Manchuria and southeastern Siberia all year long. It is larger and heavier than its better known cousin, the Bengal tiger, which is lighter in color and has thicker hair. It is, as stands to reason, one of the most dangerous animals in the world.

Not to mislead anyone about the nature of our favorite

friends, many other breeds of cats are just as at home in the cold as the Siberian tiger. There are dozens of different cat species which can handle nasty winters just fine. One of these is the non-hibernating lynx. Its broad feet enable it to travel on top of the snow and hunt game that flounders and sinks in the drifts. Another is the snow leopard, which lives among the highest ranges of the Himalayas. Even in winter it does not come down any lower than 6,000 feet.

To relieve those who may not have known this, violin strings are not made from the intestines of cats. They never were. Of course, nowadays, catgut is not used to string musical instruments; the music business has come up with a nice, synthetic replacement. By the way, catgut is not made from the intestines of cats. Catgut has always been made from the intestines of (believe it or not) sheep. Don't ask me why they ever called it catgut. That's an answer I couldn't find.

An interesting note: Large cats have litters just as house cats do. Lionesses, for example, have as many as six or seven cubs at a birth.

Another tiger fact: Like most cats, tiger young stay with their families for two years or more after their birth, after which time they are on their own. Tiger young, however, can kill their own game by the time they are seven months old.

Cat's eyes do not glow in the dark. Now, please don't yell at your book, because you know better, you've seen it happen. Believe it or not, no animal in the world has eyes that can create their own specific illumination. Cat's eyes reflect light.

The puma, the mountain lion, the panther, the painter and the catamount (as well as a few other, more obscure titles) are all names for one cat—the cougar.

The cheetah, the world's swiftest animal (officially clocked at over 70 miles an hour), is the only cat whose claws cannot be retarded or drawn into their sheaths among the pads of their feet.

Everybody knows that house cats are extremely fond of fish, and they usually don't take well to water. With both of these facts in mind, however, it's hard to believe that there is a cat which specializes in fish to such an extent that its common name is "the fishing cat." It lives in India and southern China, generally in the thickets along the edges of lakes, rivers and swamps where it 'dips' fish out of the water with what has been described as "frightening" efficiency.

One last tiger fact: Tigers seem to show individual tastes in food. Some prefer game such as deer and wild pigs. Others will feed only on cattle, horses and domesticated pigs. Still some will turn into man-eaters. Many people like to pretend that big cats only turn to man-eating when they are extremely old, or distressed, or crippled. Such is not the case with tigers. Tigers have no fear of man, and if they want something to eat that belongs to man (including man), they will simply take it. Tiger attacks have been known to account for the killing of 60,000 head of cattle, and 4,000 human beings... in just a single year!!

The Facts about Cat Myths

Cats aren't affectionate. In fact, they're cold.

To begin with, cats can be very, very affectionate (as every cat owner knows). One of the greatest pleasures a person can enjoy is cuddling a friendly cat. To paraphrase Charles Schulz, "Happiness is a Warm Kitten."

Dog owners can't begin to hug their pets the same way. Dogs simply don't "fold" as cats do when they're snuggling up to someone. You can easily embrace a (willing) cat and carry it around with you, but carrying a dog is a different story. Most dogs are bigger than most cats, and heavier.

Very often a dog expresses his affection by slurping all over someone's face. Which would you rather feel—a cat rubbing against you leg, or a sudden slurpy lick on your nose?

Cats are certainly as affectionate as dogs—they're just not as demonstrative. I once told a friend that my cats sit next to me whenever I am sick and he said, "Cats don't do that. You must be thinking of dogs."

My girlfriend's cat never lets me pet it. It always runs away when I visit her.

As for cats who won't stay around to be petted, they often sense a visitor's dislike. Many people approach a strange cat by rushing up to it and touching—or even grabbing—it. Such swift, "rude" movements always appear threatening to cats. The proper "etti-kitt" to follow calls for letting strange cats approach you first. The odds are good that it will then "get cozy" for a short while (or at least stay out in the open).

My cat didn't love me the way my dog does.

When dog owners boast that their dog loves them more than a cat could, they often refer to the services it performs for them. They assume that a dog who (let's say) guards a house, picks up papers, barks on command, etc. is expressing greater devotion than pets who don't do such things. Cats and dogs have different natures—and cats have many natural advantages over dogs. Experts know that when a cat and a dog who are both thirsty come across a faucet, it is always the cat who figures out how to turn the handle!

When I was 8 years old, I tried to play with my aunt's cat but it scratched me. Cats are vicious.

Children who "play" with cats often regard them as toys. Yanking on a cat's tail will anger the friendliest of cats, and when a cat gets angry, it's natural for it to scratch its attacker.

It's very unfortunate that many children grow up to be cat haters after a single unpleasant encounter with one. In many instances, the child isn't scratched at all, but only frightened by hissing or growling. Many cat-hating parents pass their dislike on to children with comments such as, "Stay away from cats or they'll attack you."

No one has to like cats, but it doesn't make sense to

hate them. They are certainly not nasty by nature. Parents who lie about cats to their children often do so to discourage them from asking to adopt one. It would be far better for such parents to admit that they don't want any pets around than to traumatize their child. Childhood is traumatic enough!

I once saw a barn cat playing with a mouse it caught. It kept letting it go—and then catching it again. That cat was cruel.

When cats catch mice and let them go, only to recapture them again, they are not being cruel. This activity serves to introduce their kittens to the techniques for catching prey, which can obviously be a vital skill for a cat. This is not sadism—only good parenting!

That woman is always full of gossip—she's a real cat!

Women are sometimes called "cats" but the word cat also has a positive meaning in "slanguage"—a "cool cat" is someone confident and respected.

I was petting my friend's cat and all of a sudden, for no reason at all, it tried to bite my hand!

When cats have sex, the male gently bites the female on the neck. If you're petting a cat who unexpectedly tries to bite your hand, it's very likely a tomcat with fantasizing about females. To avoid being bitten, don't stroke him too aggressively—he's agitated enough.

Cat Psychology

These days it's possible to take your cat to a pet psychiatrist, or have one make a house call. Yes, really. I'm serious. One of the jokes about them goes like this:

"Why won't you take your cat to the pet shrink?"

"He's not allowed on the couch!"

Let's face it, the idea sounds more than a little ridiculous. Dyeing your poodle so it will match your favorite outfit is one thing (one very weird thing) but having your pet psychoanalyzed is really offbeat.

Can't you just picture a cat lying on a couch, complaining:

"I wasn't my mother's favorite. She preferred her other 49 kittens over me!"

Or how about:

"I can't stand the man I'm living with. He thinks he owns me!"

Or even:

"Who's an addict? I can take catnip or leave it alone!"

Or maybe:

"I should have realized what he was up to when he asked me to meet him in the alley. But he's long gone now and I can't find a sitter for my litter!"

Or:

"I had 110 kittens. But does even one think to call or write? No!"

Or:

"I have a recurring dream—I'm in the middle of a

crowd with clothes on. Do you think it has any real meaning, doctor?"

Or:

"I can't figure it out. I know food comes from cans, but I salivate whenever I see Mickey Mouse on television. Why is that?"

Cats certainly feel deep emotions—including jealousy and homesickness—but you can usually handle them with "amateur analysis." Here are some tips to get you started:

1. Cats appreciate regular routines. For example, they like to eat their meals at the same time every day. Ideally, their meals should always be served to them by the same person, in the same place. Cats are true creatures of habit. Providing them with a set schedule will definitely give them basic peace of mind. When Edward, Miranda, Clovis and Genevieve hear the can opener roar "right on schedule" they're always thrilled—"right on schedule!"

2. A cat's territory is very important to it. Every cat (whether it's in a jungle or a home) regards its territory as something with two distinct parts. The inner part of a cat's territory (its lair) includes its sleeping area and the safe areas around it. Sometimes house cats regard "their" entire house or apartment as their lair. The outer part of a cat's territory is where it hunts or roams.

Domesticated cats that spend time outdoors may re-gard streets, backyards, garages or basements as part of their territory. In the jungle, a feline's territory usually includes hiding places, trails and places to sleep in the sun. Note: Jungle cats sleep up to two-thirds of the time—as do domestic cats!)

Cats can become quite upset if their territory isn't "respected." Many become very upset when their owners move them to new homes. If a cat isn't happy with its new home, it may return to its old one at the first available opportunity, even if it is hundreds and hundreds of miles away!

3. One way you can tell if your cat feels anxious is if it starts licking away at its fur. Just as people bite their nails when they're upset, so do cats express anxiety with similar self-destructive actions.

If your cat becomes very anxious because it's left home alone each day, you might try getting another cat to keep it company. Two cats provide excellent companionship for each other, as soon as they "decide" which one will dominate over the other.

4. If you have a house guest who brought along his cat, beware. Since most cats take more than a few days to warm up to each other, you might as well keep them apart to avoid any and all trouble. If, however, your guest and his cat are staying for more than a few days, you should introduce the two cats to each other. And, to avoid jealousy—and possibly bad behavior from your cat—pay more attention to your pet than his.

5. Cats sometimes seek attention by pretending to be sick or injured.

Even More Fascinating Facts about Cats

Dogs hunt in packs, while cats hunt alone. If you have a dog, it regards you as the leader of its pack, while your cat regards you (more or less) as "just another animal in the jungle." This explains why cats don't learn tricks as readily as dogs. A dog's instincts tell it, "Do what the leader tells you," while a cat's instincts say, "You can take care of yourself." Note: Canine breeds—such as the basenji—can be as independent as cats.

Fact has more to do with people than with cats. Many people regard their pets as their confidants because of the high degree of isolation in modern society. Since many people live by themselves these days (due to divorce, death, etc.) fewer people have close friends. Many have only "over-the-phone friendships" because they (and their friends) move so often.

It's a shame that people often turn to cats for "substitute" companionship because they can't get "the real thing"—and because cat companionship is valuable in itself. Cats lend beauty and a calming influence to any home and life.

Experts agree that cats hiss because the noise resembles the hissing made by snakes just before they strike. The sound stops most mammals in their tracks due to their instinctive fear of poisonous snakes.

Some cat books include "vocabulary lists" of cat sounds. This one doesn't. It's impossible to reproduce the wide assortment of cat sounds on paper with any real accuracy. The best way to learn cat language is to listen to your cat.

Since cats are very intelligent and every human/cat relationship is different, every cat's "vocabulary" is distinctly unique. If you listen to it closely, and pay attention to its body language, you'll soon be able to understand and communicate with your cat fluently.

A cat meows because it made that sound to attract its mother's attention when it was a kitten. Since domesticated cats regard their owners as their (new) mothers, it's only natural for them to "speak" to them as they did to their real mothers.

According to cat expert Paul Leyhausen, kittens first exhibit interest in catching prey when they're about 3 weeks old. At that age, they begin poking at small objects with their paws. Over the next few weeks they practice the essential prey-catching moves, including waiting, stalking and pouncing. If they're farm cats, their mother brings them dead mice and they become familiar with the appearance of prey. When they're ready to handle it, their mother brings them live mice.

The most important part of feline mouse-catching is "the killing bite." Cats kill by swiftly biting their prey on the neck. Kittens practice this special bite—harmlessly, obviously—on each other while they're learning.

Why are so many cats called Kitty? It's simple. Cats respond more readily to names that end with an "ee" sound. If you have to name a cat (and you want it to respond to its name) pick a short one, and be sure that it's one you won't mind yelling in the neighborhood if your cat disappears.

Fabulous Fictitious Cats

Did you know that Judy Garland once supplied the voice for a cartoon cat named Mewsette? She did it for an animated feature called *Gay Purree*, which was presented by UPA Pictures, Inc. in 1962. Garland sang several unforgettable numbers for the cartoon, including one called "Paris is a Lonely Town." Her feline swain in the movie, Jaune (Yellow) Tom, was "played" by Robert Goulet. Hermione Gingold supplied the voice for sophisticated (and jaded) Madame Rubens-Chatte, who taught Mewsette about elegance.

One of the first cats children read about is Dr. Seuss' *Cat in the Hat*, the "star" of several immensely popular children's books written in rhyme. And perhaps you remember watching the *Felix the Cat* cartoon show. In it, Felix always gets out of trouble by "reaching into his bag of tricks." Cats have always been associated with cleverness. The famous fairy tale *The Musicians of Bremen* features several animals, including a cat, that save a town.

The outrageous cat Mehitabel (created by journalist Don Marquis) represents individuals with optimism and courage. The popular comic strip cat, Garfield, on the other hand is a very cynical character. His hobbies include gobbling lasagna and tormenting his owner's other pet, a dog named Odie. Garfield's character has far less to do with cats than it does with contemporary concerns.

The millions of readers who are on diets vicariously enjoy Garfield's pasta gobbling. Many readers of Jim Davis' strip appreciate the cat's cynicism because of their own cynical views of modern times.

The term "fat cat" refers to a greedy and selfish individual. Since Garfield is fat he is, therefore, also a symbol of greed and selfishness. This symbolism makes the strip not only anti-cat, but anti-fat (people)! Its good-natured humor, though, gives it redeeming value.

In the long-running comic strip *Gasoline Alley* by Jim Scancarelli there is a character who carries a cat on his arm wherever he goes. And in *Tobermory*, a short story written by Saki (H.H. Munro), a cat who learns to speak throws a household into confusion by eavesdropping and revealing what it hears.

Many people believe that the only feline in L. Frank Baum's Oz books is the Cowardly Lion (who gains courage from helping others). The fact is that L. Frank Baum wrote many books about Oz after *The Wizard of Oz*, and two cats and a tiger appear in them. Eureka is a glass cat brought to life by a magician. The other is a pink kitten brought to Oz from Kansas by Dorothy Gale. The tiger is known as The Hungry Tiger and its chief characteristic is its strong conscience.

In the fairy tale *Puss in Boots* a cat makes its owner fabulously wealthy by tricking an ogre. He persuades the ogre to turn himself into a mouse, and then he eats it!

Cat Jokes

Have you heard about the cat that ate cheese? He wanted to wait outside a mouse hole with baited breath.

A man knocked on the door of a farmhouse and said, "I'm terribly sorry, but I accidentally ran over your cat just now. Can I replace it?" The woman said, "Sure. Can you catch mice?"

A man walked into a bar and ordered two drinks. He drank one and poured the other one into his shirt pocket. Then he ordered two more drinks and did the same thing with them. After he ordered a third round of drinks, the bartender asked him, "Why do you keep pouring drinks into your shirt pocket?" He said, "That's none of your damned business!" Just then, a mouse popped out of his pocket and snapped, "And that goes for your cat, too!"

While in the midst of preparing dinner, a man had to leave his kitchen to answer the phone. When he returned, he discovered that five pounds of roast beef were missing—and his cat looked unusually content.

He picked up the cat, carried it to a scale, and found that it weighed exactly five pounds. "There's the roast beef," he muttered, "but where's the cat?"

Catty Remarks

For some reason, there are quite a number of words and phrases still in common usage, some of them vulgar, most of them not, which include some cat related word. We all use them every day, but how many of us know where they originate from or how old they are?

"He let the cat out of the bag." This phrase dates back to the 18th century. It was the common practice during that time to take piglets to the market in small sacks. A sneak-thief trick at the time involved placing a cat inside instead, and then selling it as if it were a pig. If for some reason the thief were forced to show the contents of his bag to his market... well...

"You look like something the cat dragged in," is insulting to the cats who display their rodent "trophies" with pride. Remember, when your cat brings something to you, he regards it as both a tasty treat and an exciting example of his hunting heritage and prowess. You should be proud, too—and you should be especially proud if your cat decides to have kittens right on your bed. It means she trusts you implicitly.

"The cat must have nine lives." Cats are very hearty creatures, capable of surviving nine story falls—agile, strong, fast. Their very durability led to the belief that they had more than one life. The number nine seems to have been settled on because since ancient times it has been the trinity of trinities, the luckiest of numbers. No one has any idea how many thousands of years this belief goes back.

"There isn't room to swing a cat in here." When sailors in the first British fleets were punished, their lashes were delivered with a whip commonly referred to as the cat-o'-nine-tails. This nine-ended horror left marks on the sailor's back which resembled those from a savage cat attack. Sailors were lashed on the main deck, where there was room to use the whip.

In the year 1759 a male cat was known as a "ram." In 1760, however, a story was published entitled, *The Life and Adventures of A Cat.* The star of the story, Tom, was the star of a tremendously popular book—so popular that it wasn't long before people stopped talking about ram cats and started talking about "tom cats" instead.

"She's going to have kittens." In medieval times, a woman experiencing intense labor pains believed she wasn't having a baby at all, but a litter of kittens. Witches would have to be called in to administer a potion to ensure the woman wouldn't have kittens. Note: Until the 17th century, removing "cats in the belly" was a legal excuse for obtaining an abortion.

Since the early 1400s, common prostitutes have been referred to as cats. Cats live in a "cathouse." Pretty easy one, actually.

101

"It's raining cats and dogs outside." During the 1700s the streets were narrow and for the most part unclean. People threw their garbage out of windows and emptied chamber pots in the streets. This led to horrible conditions which clogged the sewers and caused flooding in the streets when it rained. Cats and dogs living on the garbage found in the streets would die by the dozens during the floods. Some naive members of the population actually believed the animals fell from the sky.

Now, this one may surprise you. Even the word "cat" itself is unique. The name of our favorite animal is an ancient one. The proof lies in the fact that every European and Mediterranean nation's word for cat sounds almost the same. Take a look at the following list:

Holland: Kat

France: chat

Germany: Katze

Norway: katt

Poland: kot

Italy: gatto

Spain: gato

Sweden: katt

Israel: kats

Greece: gata

The oldest use of the word which can be found comes from the area of Northern Africa—quttah. This helps to support the theory that all cats came from this region of the world after being domesticated and bred for the courts of the Pharaohs along the Nile River in Egypt.

Further proof that the cat was from this corner of the earth stems from the fact that three other words for cats, all of them equally ancient, originated in this area as well:

Turkish—kedi (kitty)
Egyptian—Pasht (puss, later pussy)
Turkish—utabi (tabby)

And, that's all we could find at the moment, but rest assured, Edward, Clovis, Miranda and Genevieve are looking for more right now.

Genevieve's Story

In return for helping me with this book, I'm giving Genevieve a chapter all her own. (Would you really believe she insisted?)

Although Gen is a beautiful silver tabby, her litter mates were all pure white (so I was told). The second I saw her it was "love at first sight."

When I introduced her to the other three cats, Edward growled, Clovis purred and Miranda licked her sides. For many months Miranda treated the newcomer as her own kitten. She groomed her all the time (occasionally holding her down with a paw in order to wash her ears). And she hissed at the males if she thought they were trying to bother her (they wouldn't dare). Eventually Miranda felt that "her kitten" was old enough to be totally independent (but she never stopped grooming her).

When Genevieve reached that stage, she began regarding me as her (main) "mother." Actually, from the moment of her arrival, she preferred my company. I think this had a lot to do with the fact that I let her sit on my lap as much as she wanted. For the first few weeks after her arrival it seemed as though she wanted to sit on my lap about 24 hours a day. When she wasn't right on me, or right next to me, she was under my bed.

Genevieve, looking over my shoulder as I type, just "said," "That's not true! I was much braver than that!" She's right. I was exaggerating. It was only 23 hours a day. Genevieve said, "Very funny!" In any case, she's as bold as can be today. Genevieve said, "That's better!"

Genevieve enjoys riding around on my shoulder. As I wrote in an earlier chapter, she often jumps onto my shoulder, without warning, from the floor. Once she's on it, she usually hangs out for a while.

Note: Cats are seldom careless with their claws. They usually don't scratch anyone or anything that they don't mean to scratch.

Cats that "wreck" furniture are just doing what comes naturally. If your cat hasn't been paying enough attention to its scratching post, try rubbing it (the post, not the cat) with catnip.

Genevieve loves to get warm in winter by lolling on top of the television. Sometimes her tail hangs down and bisects the picture. When that happens, I just put it back on top (each time she flicks it down again) until she keeps it on top. (I'm not sure, but I think, "Television Tail" is one of her favorite games.)

Whenever I take Genevieve for a walk, she always follows the same routine (of her own devising). She walks around the perimeter of the yard, never venturing into the center. I'm sure that she does this because her instincts tell her to stay hidden (or as hidden as possible).

During her walk, she inspects the same spots to see if they have any new sights or smells to offer. If she finds flowers blooming, she smells them appreciatively. When she smells something strong, she opens her mouth slightly and a look of disgust appears on her face. (This is the usual feline reaction to a strong smell.)

If she sees moths, bees or butterflies flying around, she

tries catching them. If a squirrel or a bird dares to show its face during her walk, she stares at it and gnashes her teeth. After she has completely finished her fence-hugging routine, Genevieve lies down in a cool spot to relax. Of course, if anything flies by, she's up in a flash, trying to grab it.

Genevieve and Miranda both love to get into beds while someone is trying to make them. They treat every rustle of the sheets as though it heralds the approach of a delicious mouse. (No, they have never eaten mice and are never going to.)

Genevieve used to be very frightened of the vacuum cleaner's noise and would hide whenever it was used. Now, however, she has gained enough courage to be able to watch it in operation—from a distance. Curiosity will get them every time! (Well, a lot of the time.)

When Genevieve's claws need clipping, I trim them myself. There's no reason to pay a veterinarian to do this. It's easy. The hard part is getting your cat to hold still. Genevieve doesn't normally growl, but she does whenever I start clipping her claws. When you clip them correctly, it doesn't hurt a cat at all, but the cat often resents being held in one place. (Just make sure that your cat is in a secure and comfortable position, and you will be able to clip its claws in a matter of moments.)

All you have to do is push each claw up from the bottom and quickly snip the tip without pulling on it. I keep Genevieve still by holding her front legs together in one hand. Since cats naturally rake objects with their rear legs, it's best to finish the front claws fast. Then see if you can clip the rear claws before the cat really gets annoyed. (I can usually do it.)

Edward was once taken to the veterinarian to have his claws clipped, and the vet held him near the edge of the examining table to do it. This move caused Edward to be so concerned with worrying about whether he'd fall or not that he was totally distracted from expressing resentment at the "indignity."

Many More
Fascinating Facts
about Felines

In Damon Runyon's short story, *Lillian*, the title character (a cat, of course) rescues someone from a fire. Cats frequently alert their owners to the presence of smoke in the house by nudging them awake.

Many of the novels written by the late Robert A. Heinlein center around cats. The title of his novel, *The Door into Summer*, refers to an anecdote about a cat that is described in it. A character mentions that his cat loved going outside—until the weather turned cold. When it did, the cat led him from one door to another until he had opened all of them. This convinced him that the cat was looking for (you guessed it) "the door into summer."

Another Heinlein novel, entitled *The Cat Who Walked through Walls*, features a cat whose ability to escape from any room earns it the nickname in the title.

In a *Star Trek* episode, a witch demonstrates the ability to turn herself into a black cat. In the movie *Bell, Book and Candle*, starring Jimmy Stewart and Kim Novak, Novak plays a witch who has a feline familiar named "Pyewacket."

Jungle cats and domesticated cats often move their kittens from the "nest" a few days after they're born. When mother cats carry their kittens, they hold them gently by the backs of their necks. When they hold them that way, the kittens become rigid and easier for them to carry. (Remember the "Spock pinch" on *Star Trek*? The Vulcan technique that enabled Spock to disable his enemies with one touch? This kitten carrying technique is very similar to that imaginary one.)

A cat once "starred" in an episode of *Mission: Impossible*. It helped the team by walking on a board when it was cued.

The Koreans regard the tiger as "the King of Beasts." If the lion is the King of Beasts, isn't there an "Earl of Beasts" or a "Baron of Beasts?" Just wondering. Seriously, the lion doesn't deserve the title King of Beasts because it's the lioness that does the hunting. The phrase "the lion's share" is accurate, however (it refers to the largest share of anything), because lions always try to grab the largest share of the meat!

A naturalist named Joy Adamson was able to raise a lioness from a cub and train it to return to the wild. Adamson related her experiences in a book, *Born Free*, which was later made into a successful movie. She also wrote two sequels to it, *Living Free* and *Forever Free*.

Cats, a popularly acclaimed Broadway musical, has been running for years. It's interesting to note that there has never been a Broadway success entitled "Dogs!"

Female cats ovulate instantly when they mate.

When your cat dies, you can take it to one of the many pet cemeteries in the United States, and have a special gravestone made for it. Or, you can have its body preserved with a new freeze-drying method. The freeze-drying method removes most of the moisture from the body. Animal bodies preserved with this method supposedly last longer that those preserved with more traditional taxidermy methods.

An Assortment of Thoughts and Advice about Cats

Never, never, never have a cat declawed. One reason is because if a declawed house cat should happen to get out, it's doomed. Without claws a cat cannot defend itself against an attacker, or climb a tree to escape. As I wrote in an earlier chapter, clipping a cat's claws takes only moments once you've gotten the knack.

If you ask someone why he loves his pet, the answer is usually not, "I love its silky fur" or "Animals are so interesting to watch." The popular reply is, "It doesn't answer back!"

Cats spray by backing up to a vertical object and releasing a spray of urine. Most often this is done by males (to mark their territory) but females do it, too. When cats spray, it's akin to putting up a signboard that says, "This is the territory of..." Depending on the season, the signboard can also read, "I am looking for a female cat" or "I am looking for a tomcat." Cats sometimes spray to express anxiety.

If you're planning to adopt a cat, how about adopting an older one from a shelter? They are more sedate and already know all about using litter boxes. Most importantly, older cats are often passed over in favor of kittens.

When that happens, shelters usually eliminate them right away to make room for new arrivals.

Thousands and thousands of unwanted cats arrive at shelters each year—and die there—for the following reasons:

1. People who say, "I want my cat to have kittens so that my children can witness the miracle of birth." If you want your children to see the birth process, consider these arguments against it:

A. The cat could have stillborn kittens or a difficult labor. Witnessing such events could traumatize children.

B. If (as usually happens) you cannot find homes for the kittens and are forced to take them to a shelter (which is forced to destroy them), your children will be upset. Such an action will negate your intended message about the sacredness of life.

2. People who say, "I like to play with kittens, but when they grow up, I become bored with them." If you know someone who only cares for his pets as long as they stay cute, tell them to get hamsters instead of cats. Hamsters never get bigger.

A cat known as "Fat Freddy's Cat" was featured in several issues of a popular underground comic book series.

One of the Disney films that featured cats was *The Nine Lives of Thomasina*. The cat with the title role had many adventures, and even visited "cat heaven" in a surreal sequence.

Recently, on the television show, *America's Funniest Home Videos*, the winning videotape featured a cat falling off of a television set. A similar fall by a human would be nothing to laugh at, but cats have a truly amazing ability to land on their feet. Cats flip around instinctively in mid-air like well-trained acrobats. Cats have fallen from heights of over nine stories and survived.

Sometimes cats purr so loudly from fear when they're being examined by veterinarians that only purring can be heard through the stethoscope!

Questions and Answers

At this point I'd like to take the time to gather up all the odd snippets and bits that aren't really "facts" and don't quite make it as chapters. Hopefully, you will find them as noteworthy as I do.

As many of you already know, the Egyptians worshipped their cats. They constructed gods with the heads of cats, mummified their furpals at the time of their deaths and even mummified mice for them to eat in the afterlife. Their love of cats knew no bounds.

A Roman soldier was once torn limb from limb by outraged Egyptians for the crime of merely harming a cat. The cat lived... he didn't.

Any Egyptian who killed a cat was automatically condemned to death. An attacking army (ironically, an army of Persians!) once forced an Egyptian city to surrender by supplying its soldiers with cats. Since the Egyptians would never risk hurting them (the cats, of course, not the soldiers!) they had no choice but to surrender.

Roman soldiers were responsible for introducing cats into Europe. They brought cats with them on their campaigns across Europe—cats that they had illegally appropriated from the Egyptians.

Also, transporting cats out of Egypt was considered a major offense. The ancient Phoenicians, in the fashion of modern drug runners, made catnapping one of their standard practices, smuggling cats out of Egypt for sale to rich pet owners throughout the known world!

As long as we are on the subject of the ancient world, let's look at something else. The dog has changed considerably since he was first domesticated. But remarkably, the cat has not. Most changes in the cat have been superficial. Dogs are greatly reduced in stature and power from their ancestors, but not cats. The length of their coats and the amount of times a year they breed (up from one to three) is about all the changes that have occurred over the years.

Many people feel that cats bury their feces as carefully as they do because they are the most fastidious of creatures. As beautiful as this myth is, it is not the truth.

In the wild, only subordinate cats bury their waste products. The dominant personality in any area will prominently display his feces, always in the open, on a hilltop if possible.

In the modern home, the master/mistress of the house is the dominant personality. So as not to offend either, house cats will carefully bury their feces to eliminate interference with what they perceive as the natural order.

Cats will both hiss and spit when they are attacked or feel threatened. Why do they do this? Believe it or not, they are imitating snakes! The sound of a cat's hiss is almost a perfect mimicry of the sound of a snake's. Since many snakes spit as well, cats added that to their repertoire over the centuries as well.

One characteristic many people have wondered about is why cats play with their prey. Why, they want to know, when a cat has cornered a helpless mouse, does it torture it endlessly until the beast finally dies of fright? Why don't they just finish it off and be done with it? Why, they want to know, must cats be so cruel?

The truth is, the cat is not being cruel at all. First off, these are actions of domesticated cats. Field cats living off what they catch will kill their prey and eat it immediately. House cats, however, are well fed. They have no need to devour their prey instantly. Also, they do not hunt every day, or every week, or even every month. Many house cats do not see a mouse more than once or twice a year.

When they do catch one, they cannot bear for the hunt to end. It is an event, one which they drag on to the bitter end to help satisfy their strong hunting instinct. Also, female cats have a responsibility to teach their young to hunt. Females with kittens will bring live prey back to their young and instruct them in the finer points of stalking their own food.

For years we have heard stories of lost cats finding their way back home, even though they were hundreds of miles away. Are these stories true, and what can account for this near miraculous ability?

Yes, the stories are true. It seems that cats (as well as many other mammals, including human beings) possess an extraordinary sensitivity to the earth's magnetic poles. This ability allows them to find their way home with no external clues at all.

Many people (especially if they have been reading this chapter) are aware that the Egyptians worshipped cats. But during medieval times, cats were destroyed as witches' familiars. The question no one seems to ask is, when did things swing back? If cats were persecuted almost to extinction, when did they return to current favor as the world's most popular house pet?

The answer is the Victorian era. It was not until the 1800s that the cat again became a house pet with greater frequency. The sentimental Victorians became enamored with cats, bringing about the return of their popularity. Now they outnumber dogs and, at least unofficially, have inherited the title of "man's best friend" from the canine.

Which do Americans buy more of... cat food or baby food? Do you really have to ask? Cat food, of course. More than $2 billion worth a year.

Here is a really odd one for those who don't already know it. A litter of kittens can have more than one father. It's true. Cat sex is not a long, drawn out affair. A female in heat will be mounted by a male for a period of only seconds. Once he is finished, however, this does not mean his partner is. The female will more often than not

remain in an inviting position, allowing one male after another to mount her. After that, it is anyone's guess which sperm fertilized which egg.

This, of course, can result in litters with a wide variety of kittens, as varied, or even moreso, than the fathers involved. But more bizarre than this, however, is the female cat's ability to go into heat while she is already pregnant! True... a female cat can get the urge to mate while already carrying a litter, and then end up pregnant again, carrying two litters at the same time at two different stages of development!

And, as long as we are on the topic, I might as well mention that cats can continue to have litters into their 16th year—the equivalent of a human female being able to give birth in her late 60s. Tomcats can sire a litter into their 17th year—the equivalent of a human male suddenly becoming a daddy in his late 70s.

Getting back to more delicate matters, there seems to be some confusion as to when cat shows first began. Some people say the 1500s; others say the date of the first cat show was in the 1800s. Both answers are correct.

The reason for this is that yes, there were cat shows in the 1500s, but they were small shows with little meaning. Breeding meant nothing in those days. The cat was not the varied, handsome animal the Victorians raised in the 1800s, when people began having the type of cat shows that are familiar today.

120

Lastly, I'd just like to let you know what good company you are in. The cat has always been a highly prized pet of the rich and famous. Here is a small list of some of the world's most important cat owners throughout history: Cleopatra... Edward Lear (the Victorian artist and author)...Sir Isaac Newton... Dr. Samuel Johnson... Edgar Allen Poe... Theophile Gautier (the French novelist and poet)... Charles Dickens... Ichijo (an early Japanese emperor)... Karel Capek (the Czech playwright)... Theodore Roosevelt... Mark Twain... the great prophet Mohammed... and, of course, you!!

Letters to Dear Tabby

Dear Tabby:

I am a white Persian that just had a litter. My two kittens each have one blue eye and one brown eye. Is this unusual?

Purry Persian

Dear Purry:

Congratulations on your new additions! What you describe is not unusual. The combination has no effect on a cat's vision, so there's no reason to worry. In fact, you should be glad that your kittens don't have two blue eyes—white Persians with blue eyes are often deaf.

Dear Tabby:

I love sniffing catnip! In fact, when I get really excited, I chew on it. Could I become addicted to it?

Worried

Dear Worried:

Don't worry, catnip is nowhere near as damaging as marijuana. However, you'll enjoy it more if you only smell it once in a while.

Dear Tabby:

My owner—I mean, my human pet—doesn't understand that I'm very fastidious. I want him to change my litter box every day (or at least clean it out) but he doesn't. What can I do? If he doesn't start cleaning it more pretty soon, I'm going to start urinating in the corner of his room!

Desperate

Dear Desperate:

Stop! Don't do anything drastic yet! Just show him this column and he'll get the message.

Dear Tabby:

I've had three litters of kittens and raised them all by myself. It's not easy feeding them, protecting them and teaching them what they have to know. Why are tomcats such lousy parents?

Overworked

Dear Overworked:

If it's any consolation to you, jungle cats act just the way tomcats do. They usually leave the hunting and the cub-raising to lionesses and pay little attention to family matters. It's just as well, though—lions have been known to eat their own cubs, if they get hungry enough!

Dear Tabby:

My human insists on dressing me up for special occasions and I hate it! How can I talk her out of doing this? (For her Valentine's Day party, she dressed me in a little diaper and said I was Cupid! (I shook it off right away!)

Clothescat

Dear Clothescat:

Tell your human that you don't need to wear any clothes, no matter what they look like, because you were born with a fur coat—and it has a lifetime guarantee!

Dear Tabby:

I see a lot of commercials on television for various cat foods and I would like to know which one is the best. Can you help me?

Couch Potato Cat

Dear Couch:

(If you're a feline couch potato, are you a potato with slanted eyes? Just wondering.) In answer to your question, tell your human to look carefully at the labels of the foods he buys you. (And to look carefully at the labels of the foods he buys himself.) Also, tell him that you like both dry food and canned food (and appropriate treats from the table, too!)

You might also tell your human that cats like to "snack" on and off all day (and that doing the same thing would probably be good for his health).

Dear Tabby:

My human always pushes me out of my favorite chair when he gets home! What can I do about this?

Annoyed

Dear Annoyed:

Don't do anything—humor him. (The fact that he prefers your favorite chair shows he has good taste.)

Dear Tabby:

I love to roam around outdoors, but no one can tell who I am when I'm exploring. How can I get my human to give me a collar with my name one it? (I come from a very aristocratic—or rather, aristocatic—background and I want the whole world to know my family name.)

Anonymous

Dear Tabby:

Show your human this column and be sure to tell him to get you a collar that will slip off easily in case of an emergency. Don't let him buy you one with a buckle on it! (Tell him they're not your style.)

Dear Tabby:

I met my human when I was given to her as a birthday present. She wasn't expecting an addition to her household and I don't feel very welcome in her home. What can I do?

Feeling Rejected

Dear Feeling:

Humans can be so thoughtless. When will they learn that animals aren't toys, and shouldn't be given to people who aren't expecting them? The best thing you two can do is to "get an annulment." Ideally, she'll find you a home where you'll really be appreciated. Good luck!

Dear Tabby:

My human went away for the summer and left me in the backyard. When can I expect him back? I'm getting really hungry.

Wondering

Dear Wondering:

I sincerely hope another human takes you to an animal shelter soon. If that doesn't happen, you'll be in a lot of trouble, I'm afraid. (Let me know how you manage. I care!)

Dear Tabby:

I really can't understand humans. For example, when they have newspapers, they hold them up in front of themselves for long periods without ever playing with them.

They would rather watch a box full of flickering lights for hours than a mouse hole. (That's crazy!)

They eat foods I would never touch, the male ones regularly shave their whiskers off their faces... the list of strange things goes on and on. Has anyone ever analyzed their strange behavior?

Puurplexed

Dear Puurplexed:

Humans are very strange, but as I've said before, it's best to humor them. After all, well-trained ones make excellent household pets and servants.

Dear Tabby:

I'm only four months old and I just heard that my human is getting a puppy! What should I do? I've always heard that cats and dogs tend to get along like—well—cats and dogs.

Scared

Dear Scared:

You have nothing to worry about. Cats and dogs often become firm friends. The new arrival will likely become your "bodyguard" and the best friend you ever had!

Dear Tabby:

I am a black cat, and I am sick and tired of hearing people say that I bring bad luck. Where did that ridiculous idea start, anyway?

Fed Up

Dear Fed:

Unfortunately, you face a "double whammy." The color black has often been associated with evil, and so have cats. Fortunately, though, fewer people believe in silly superstitions such as that one these days. (Be glad you weren't born in the Middle Ages. Cats were sometimes burned at the stake then!)

Dear Tabby:

My girlfriend is having kittens and I suspect that I'm not the father of her expected litter! What should I do?

Jealous

Dear Jealous:

Relax. You're undoubtedly the father of some of her (future) kittens. Nature gave cats the ability to have litters with more than one father. You have to agree that this ability is invaluable (in regard to perpetuating the feline species efficiently).

Dear Tabby:

I like to chew on my owner's blankets. Am I strange?

Bedbug

Dear Bedbug:

You're not strange, just nostalgic. Chewing on blankets reminds cats of the happy days when they were being raised by their mother. If it's any consolation, humans do similar things. Many of them derive comfort and confidence from chewing on things such as sticks of gum, cigars and pipes.

Dear Tabby:

When I'm defending myself (against "play" attacks from other cats), I sometimes lie on my back. Am I crazy? I can't understand why I'm prompted to make this move. After all, it exposes me to attack—doesn't it?

Fighter

Dear Fighter:

You're not crazy. It's true that lying on your back exposes your vulnerable stomach area to the world. But cats have a long tradition of raking enemies with their hind legs, so the "exposure" really serves as "bait" to trick an opponent into being kicked. (Good strategy, eh?)

Dear Tabby:

I often see jungle cats pacing in their cages at the zoo. Why do they do that?

Jungle Cat Fan

Dear Fan:

They do it because they're bored, bored, bored! Very often jungle cats imprisoned in old-fashioned cages at zoos go half-insane from lack of stimulation.

Fortunately, many zoos now have "natural habitat areas" instead of dreary cages for their inhabitants. These areas are a tremendous improvement over the enclosures from "the bad old days."

Dear Tabby:

My human is away from home for most of each day. Where does he go?

Curious

Dear Curious:

He goes to work so he can afford to buy cat food, veterinarian visits and other things for you. Note: This is definitely what many cats think. Ask any cat owner!

Dear Tabby:

I nap for most of each day. When I'm not sleeping, I'm eating or playing. Tell me, Tabby—what's my problem?

Too Happy

Dear Too:

It's regrettable that you don't live in the jungle, where danger lurks at every turn, or in an alley, where undernourished cats survive by disemboweling diseased rodents. But, that's life.

Dear Tabby:

I recently lost my tail. Where can I get a new one?

Missing A Tail

Dear Missing:

The retail store, where else?

Dear Tabby:

I get annoyed whenever I see the *Heathcliff* comic strip. Its star is a cat, but he's always depicted as a fish robber and troublemaker. Why don't I ever see any good cat characters?

Good Guy

Dear Good:

Publisher William Randolph Hearst (a human) once said, "Controversy sells newspapers." It is also responsible for selling comic strips, television shows, movies, books, magazines and so on.

Dear Tabby:

What kind of a cat are you?

Fan

Dear Fan:

I'm a Siamese (twin). Both my sister and I write advice columns. (Her column is only for singles—it's called Man Landers.)

Dear Tabby:

How many cats does it take to screw in a light bulb?

Joker

Dear Joker:

Why would a cat want to screw in a light bulb? Cats can see in the dark.

Dear Tabby:

I'm orange, black and white, and my fiancée is black, gray and white. If we got married, do you think we would clash?

Engaged

Dear Engaged:

It depends. Are you thinking about your marriage or your color scheme?

Dear Tabby:

My human recently brought home a little kitten and it's getting much more attention than I am. Why do humans think kittens are so cute?

Grumpy

Dear Grumpy:

Babies that have big eyes and "babyish" features (including baby humans, baby cats and baby dogs) make humans say "Awwww, isn't it cute!"—and make animals react similarly. The perception of "cuteness" (in other words, helplessness and harmlessness) stimulates humans and animals to act protectively. This reaction helps keep the human race (and animal species) going. Note: Incidentally, the cuteness of many grown men and women is related to "natural cuteness." The features that many men like to see in women—enlarged eyes, round cheeks, small noses—are an infant's features.

Dear Tabby:

Why can't cats swim? (Nyahh, nyahh!)

Dog Paddler

Dear Dog:

Who needs to get wet when you're always well-groomed? (Nyahh, nyahh!)

Dear Tabby:

I like vegetables. Should I become a vegetarian?

Health Cat

Dear Health Cat:

Eating vegetables (and grains) is all right once in a while, but you cannot become a vegetarian—cats need meat.

Dear Tabby:

What time do you get up in the morning?

Late Sleeper

Dear Late:

Furry early!

Dear Tabby:

Why are cats so attracted to catnip?

Mellow Meower

Dear Mellow:

Catnip contains a substance called nepetalactone, which is attractive to almost two-thirds of all domestic cats. Scientists aren't exactly sure why cats are excited by it, but they know that it is related to the marijuana plant. Over-using catnip changes a cat's personality, just as abusing marijuana changes a human's personality.

Some cats sit and stare after sniffing catnip and others energetically rub their faces in it. Cats don't become attracted to it until after they're two months old.

Dear Tabby:

How fast can cheetahs run?

Marathon Cat

Dear Marathon:

Cheetahs can accelerate up to 45 miles per hour in three seconds, and reach nearly 65 miles per hour two seconds later. (A particularly fast race horse can run only about 50 miles per hour.) It can only run that fast for a few hundred yards.

Cheetahs (like lions and other big cats) greet each other by rubbing cheeks. Cheetah mothers and their cubs stay away from other adult cheetahs, and adult female cheetahs stay away from each other. Cheetah mothers are excellent at teaching their cubs how to hunt.

Dear Tabby:

Tell me the facts about lions that aren't commonly known.

Scholar

Dear Scholar:

A lion can eat up to 60 pounds of food at one time, but when it does, it doesn't eat again for several days. A pride (group) of lions can have up to 35 members. Believe it or not, lions are good swimmers.

Dear Tabby:

What's the strangest cat in the world?

Weirdo

Dear Weirdo:

I'd say it was the Pallas Cat, which lives in Central Asia, Kashmir, Tibet and Mongolia. It looks unlike any other kind of cat (wild or domestic) because its eyes are set high up in its head, and it has stout legs and an unusually heavy coat. The Pallas Cat's ability to peer over rocks and its coloration serve as camouflage when it's hunting. It eats rodents, reptiles, birds and rabbits.

Dear Tabby:

You know all sorts of amazing things! Tell me more!

Big Fan

Dear Big:

Here goes. When a male tiger sprays his territory, he's conveying the message, "Welcome, girls! Males, keep out or else!"

Tigers can eat 45 to 60 pounds of meat at one sitting.

In the early 1920s, there were about 45,000 tigers in India. By 1964 only 3,000 remained. Their numbers diminished because of indiscriminate hunting and poisoned traps.

Tigers are almost extinct in China because the Chinese believe that almost every part of their bodies is good for making medication.

A Cat's Tale

Genevieve here! While my human's away from the type-writer, I'm going to spill some deep secrets about feline body language.

My human was right when she said a cat's vocabulary is so complex that you can't describe it simply. Everything I "say" is conveyed with various combinations of glances, twitches, movements, meows and tail motions. But I'm going to tell you a lot about tail movements that should go a long way towards helping you to understand "cat language."

When I'm happy and content, I let my tail lie flat on the floor and allow the end to twitch now and then. (When I do this in my sleep, my human sometimes touches my tail and causes me to curl it up. She's surprised that I can react that way in my sleep, but the joke's on her—I'm not fully asleep then!) If something gets my attention, I move my tail a little more. This always means, "Hmmmm. What's going on? I think it sounds interesting."

Basically, when my tail is vertical (or almost vertical) I'm happy, healthy, energetic, curious, playful—or all of the above. When my tail is hanging down, I'm unhappy, anxious, upset, ill—or all of the above. If I press my tail between my hind legs, it means, "I surrender!" or "You're the boss!" (I never do that myself but there are cats around here that do—I'm not mentioning any names, but you could ask Edward or Clovis what they know!)

Edward here! I resent that insinuation! I only made a gesture like that once, and I was at a veterinarian's office at the time. That's a frightening place, no doubt about it!

Genevieve here! As I was about to say, courageous cats swish their tails back and forth before they attack. Cats that are totally confused about how to behave often start grooming themselves. Psychiatrists (for humans) refer to this as a displacement activity. Humans who scratch their heads when they're thinking are expressing confusion about a problem. Other examples of humans who employ displacement activities include those who fuss with their hair when they're worried and who crack their knuckles when they're anxious.

Oops, gotta go! My human's coming back!

Final Facts

(Hmmm, where did that last chapter come from? I must have typed it up and then forgotten about it. Genevieve and Edward couldn't have typed it... could they?)

The following are some final facts:

Mark Twain said a lot of things about cats, including this quote: "A cat that once sits on a hot stove-lid will never sit on one again... but it won't sit on a cold one, either."

Cats can't tell the difference between a sugar solution and water with nothing in it.

Aesop, the famous fable writer, wrote several stories about cats. Perhaps the most famous one involves a group of mice who organize themselves into a committee, which unanimously decides to attach a bell to the local cat. Once this decision is made, however, they argue endlessly about just who will do the dangerous deed!

Cats have an inner eyelid, which is called the haw. It sometimes slides partially over their eyes while they're asleep, and it is sometimes visible in cats who are undernourished (and awake).

Siegfried and Roy, two men who have a very successful wild animal act, own (among other felines) a rare white tiger. When it recently gave birth, it had its cubs in a place it considered very secure—the bedroom of one of the performers!

Recently, a cat belonging to Gary Brodsky of Brooklyn, New York knocked the telephone receiver off the hook when it was ringing—and said, "Meow!" into the mouthpiece.

Harlan Ellison, the tremendously popular author/journalist/television writer, wrote a story entitled, "A Boy and His Dog," and dedicated it to his dog, Ahbhu. This book is dedicated to my favorite cat, Genevieve.